AIR COMBAT 1945

The Aircraft of World War II's Final Year

Donald Nijboer

STACKPOLE
BOOKS

Copyright © 2015 by Donald Nijboer

Published by
STACKPOLE BOOKS
5067 Ritter Road
Mechanicsburg, PA 17055
www.stackpolebooks.com

Printed in the United States of America

10 9 8 7 6 5 4 3 2 1

Cover design by Caroline Stover

Library of Congress Cataloging-in-Publication Data

Nijboer, Donald, 1959–
    Air combat 1945 : the aircraft of World War II's final year / Donald Nijboer.
        pages cm. — (Stackpole military photo series)
    ISBN 978-0-8117-1606-2
1. World War, 1939–1945—Aerial operations—Pictorial works. 2. Airplanes, Military—History—20th century—Pictorial works. I. Title.
    D785.N55 2015
    940.54'4—dc23
                                                            2015012452

CONTENTS

CHAPTER 1

GREAT BRITAIN

Shortly after dawn on January 1, 1945, the Luftwaffe unleashed 986 single-seat fighters, including twenty-four Me 262s, against Allied tactical airfields in Operation *Bodenplatte.* No. 439 Squadron RCAF was one of the victims, with a number of Typhoons destroyed at its Eindhoven base.

A Halifax Mk III of No. 420 Squadron RCAF prepares for takeoff in January 1945. The aircraft is equipped with a single .50-caliber machine gun in its ventral Preston-Green turret. Starting in December 1943, No. 420 Squadron was equipped with Halifaxes and flew them until the end of the war. In the squadron's last successful mission of World War II, eighteen Halifaxes bombed Heligoland. DND

A Halifax Mk III of No. 426 Squadron at dispersal. Based at Linton-on-Ouse, No. 426 Squadron flew as part of No. 6 Group RCAF and was equipped with both the Halifax Mk III and Mk VII from April 1944 until May 1945. The squadron lost 36 aircraft in 149 bombing operations. DND

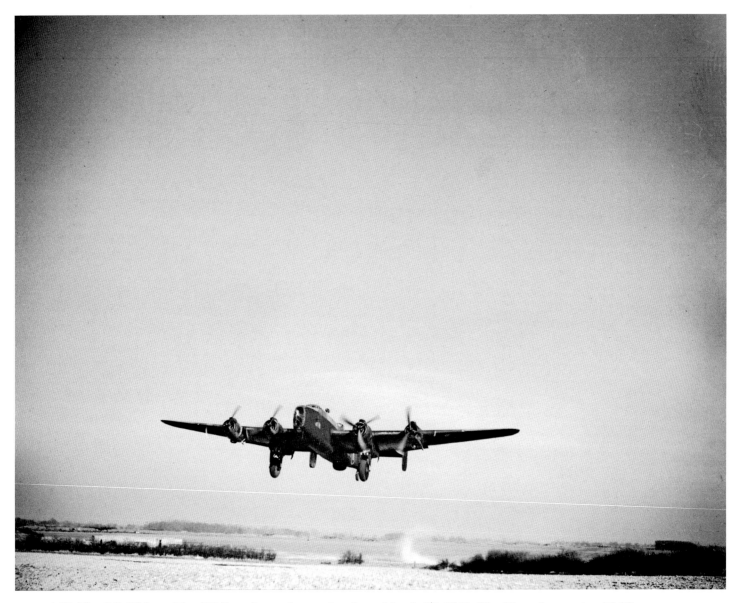

A Halifax Mk III from No. 426 Squadron takes to the air on March 17, 1945. The Hercules–engine Halifax proved as resilient as it was popular—four of these aircraft finished the war with more than 100 operational missions over Germany. Frequently overshadowed by the well-known Avro Lancaster, the Halifax's huge contribution to Bomber Command's war effort is often forgotten. At its peak, the Halifax force comprised 35 squadrons with 1,500 aircraft. DND

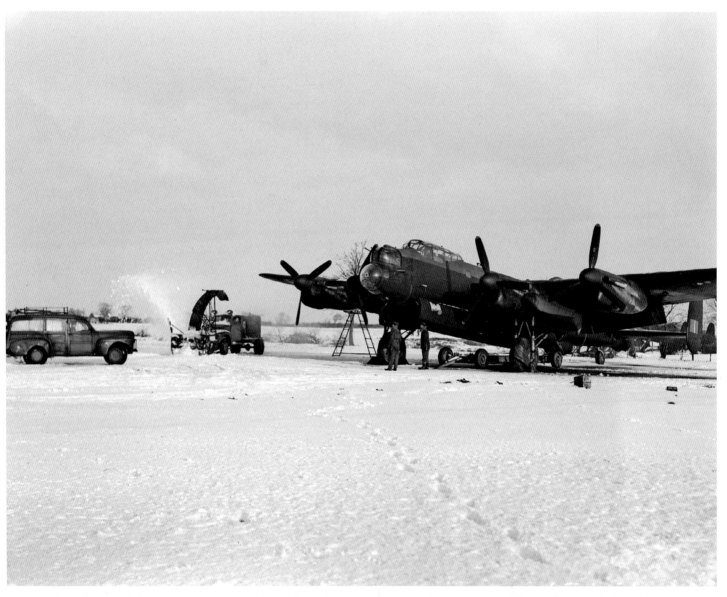

A Canadian-built Mk X Lancaster of No. 419 Squadron RCAF snowed in on January 11, 1945. A total of 430 Mk Xs were built in Canada, with No. 419 Squadron receiving its first example in early 1944. In June 1945 the squadron flew its Lancasters back to Canada and was disbanded three months later. DND

Lancaster KB-732 VR-X, *X-Terminator*, of No. 419 Squadron RCAF, with its bomb log of seventy-five operational sorties proudly painted on the nose. No. 6 Group RCAF flew 40,822 sorties during the course of the war with a loss of 4,272 aircrew killed in operations. DND

April 5, 1945. Two Lancaster Mk Xs of No. 419 Squadron RCAF on the ground at Middleton St-George, Durham. On April 25, No. 419 Squadron flew its last mission of the war, with fifteen Lancasters bombing the gun batteries on the island of Wangerooge. DND

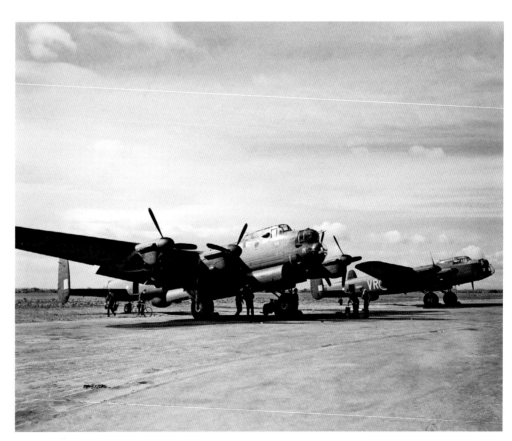

Nineteen Lancasters of No. 617 "Dambusters" Squadron attack the railway viaduct at Arnsberg on March 19, 1945. Six dropped the massive 22,000-pound Grand Slam bomb and the remainder dropped the 12,000-pound Tallboy bomb. A 40-foot (12-meter) gap was blown out of the viaduct and the structure was severely damaged. DND

April 1945. A No. 617 Squadron RAF Lancaster Mk I (Special) is bombed up with a single 22,000-pound Grand Slam bomb. To improve accuracy, the Lancasters of No. 617 Squadron were equipped with the new gyro-stabilized SABS (Stabilized Automatic Bombsight). Only the Lancaster was capable of carrying the Grand Slam; with a regular bomb load, it could carry 14,000 pounds over a range of 1,040 miles. DND

This impressive aerial photograph shows twelve Lancasters of No. 428 "Ghost" Squadron RCAF lined up nose to tail on May 31, 1945, the day they left for Canada. Eight RCAF squadrons, including No. 428, had been selected to participate in the war against Japan as part of Tiger Force. DND

LEFT: Toward the end of 1944, Bomber Command was planning daylight operations over Germany. The need for turrets armed with heavy-caliber guns was given priority. In response, Nash & Thompson produced the FN82 tail turret in 1945. Armed with two .50-caliber machine guns, it was further enhanced by the deadly Mk IID gyro gunsight and a radar blind-firing system.

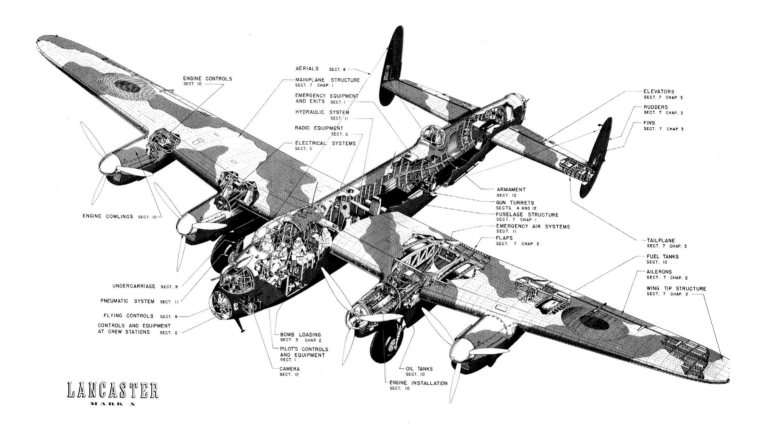

ENGINE CONTROLS
SECT. 10

AERIALS   SECT. 6

MAINPLANE STRUCTURE
SECT. 7 CHAP. 1

EMERGENCY EQUIPMENT
AND EXITS   SECT. 1

HYDRAULIC SYSTEM
SECT. 11

RADIO EQUIPMENT
SECT. 6

ELECTRICAL SYSTEMS
SECT. 5

ELEVATORS
SECT. 7 CHAP. 3

RUDDERS
SECT. 7 CHAP. 3

FINS
SECT. 7 CHAP. 3

ENGINE COWLINGS SECT. 10

ARMAMENT
SECT. 12

GUN TURRETS
SECTS. 4 AND 12

FUSELAGE STRUCTURE
SECT. 7 CHAP. 1

EMERGENCY AIR SYSTEMS
SECT. 11

FLAPS
SECT. 7 CHAP. 2

TAILPLANE
SECT. 7 CHAP. 3

FUEL TANKS
SECT. 10

AILERONS
SECT. 7 CHAP. 2

WING TIP STRUCTURE
SECT. 7 CHAP. 2

UNDERCARRIAGE SECT. 9

PNEUMATIC SYSTEM SECT. 11

FLYING CONTROLS   SECT. 8

CONTROLS AND EQUIPMENT
AT CREW STATIONS   SECT. 2

BOMB LOADING
SECT. 3 CHAP. 2

PILOT'S CONTROLS
AND EQUIPMENT
SECT. 1

CAMERA
SECT. 12

OIL TANKS
SECT. 10

ENGINE INSTALLATION
SECT. 10

LANCASTER
MARK X

The Lancaster Mk X was the Canadian version of the famous Avro bomber. Built by Victory Aircraft in Malton, it differed from the English version in a number of ways. The engines installed were Packard–built Merlin 38s or 224s, and all instruments and radio equipment were of Canadian or American manufacture. The first Lancaster Mk Xs had Frazer-Nash–manufactured mid-upper turrets. After the 168th machine had been produced, these were replaced by the U.S.–built, electrically powered Martin mid-upper turret with two .50-caliber machine guns. A total of 430 Mk X Lancasters were built, and 100 lost to all causes.

Direct hit. This is one of a handful of photographs that show an aircraft blowing up in midair. This No. 3 Group Lancaster was lost, mostly likely to a direct hit by flak, over Wesel on February 19, 1945. Of the 168 Lancasters sent out, it was the only one shot down.

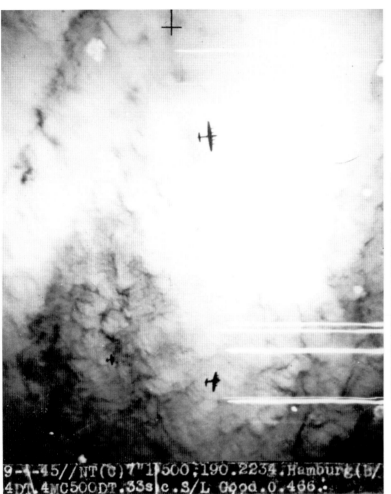

This is one of very few bombing photographs that actually show a night fighter (Ju 88) in pursuit of what appears to be a Lancaster bomber (the original caption for the photograph identifies the aircraft as a Halifax, but the rounded wing tips suggest a Lancaster). The top bomber looks more like a Halifax. This photo was taken during the last major raid of the war on Hamburg, April 8/9, 1945.

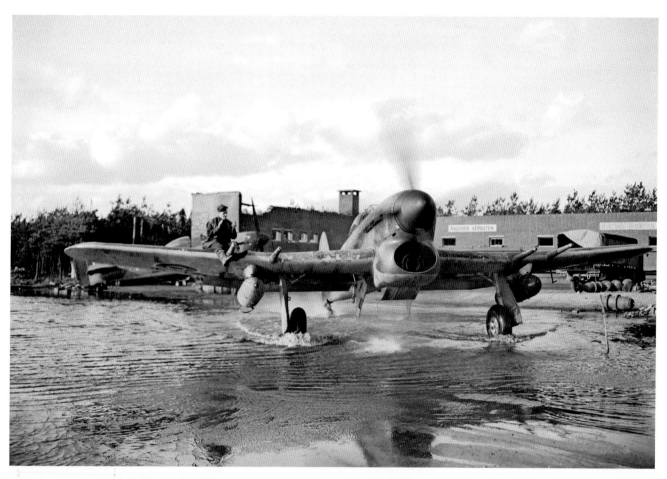

A Typhoon of No. 439 Squadron RCAF at B.78 (Eindhoven) taxis out for another mission in March 1945. This view suggests the heavyweight status of the Typhoon, which is armed with two 1,000-pound bombs. Its empty and loaded weights were 8,690 and 11,780 pounds, respectively. A Spitfire Mk IX was 7,300 pounds loaded, while a P-51D Mustang came in at 9,200 pounds. DND

Stuck in the mud. A No. 143 Wing RCAF Typhoon needs assistance after taxiing off the perimeter track at Eindhoven in March 1945. Even with its massive twenty-four-cylinder Sabre engine, this Typhoon still required some manhandling to get it back on track. DND

A No. 247 "China British" Squadron rocket projectile–equipped Typhoon takes off on another mission. Each rocket projectile (RP) weighed in at about 90 pounds. Rockets were a "one-shot" weapon and inaccurate. Although famed as "tank busters," the Typhoons of the 2nd Tactical Air Force destroyed very few tanks during the European campaign. After the battle of Falaise, Operational Research officers concluded that the RPs had been disappointing against armor. DND

By late January 1945 most single-seat fighters in the 2nd Tactical Air Force had been equipped with the new GM2 gyro gunsight. A major step forward in air-to-air gunnery, this gunsight gave the "average" fighter pilot a much better chance of scoring hits and making kills.

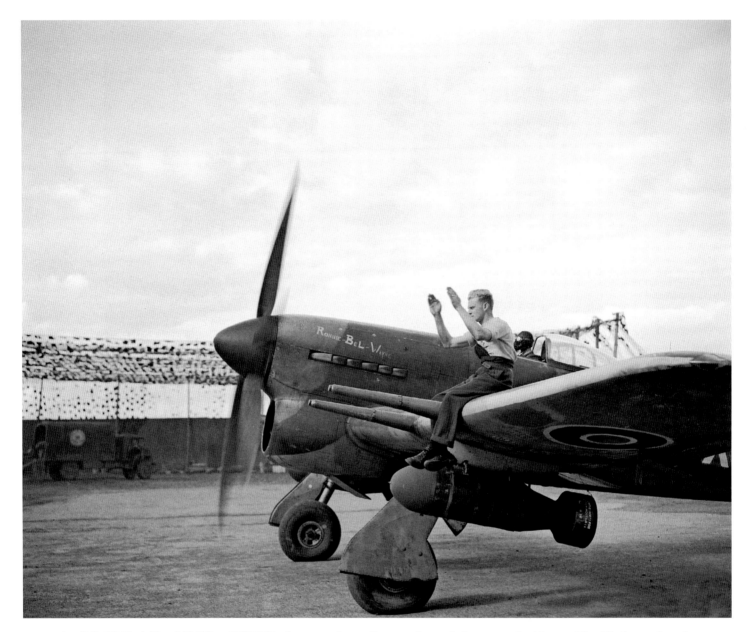

April 2, 1945. A No. 143 Wing RCAF Typhoon taxis out for another mission armed with two No. 23 cluster bombs with the streamlined nose. These comprised 26-by-20-pound fragmentation bombs that did not always perform as advertised. Problems with units failing to disintegrate were experienced due to unstable flight or damage to the tail unit when released. DND

MN606 ZY-T of No. 247 Squadron undergoes servicing in one of the wrecked hangars at B.78 (Eindhoven).
Without adequate shelter, maintenance had to done in the great outdoors, no matter what the conditions. Here,
two crewmen work on the always-demanding Sabre engine.

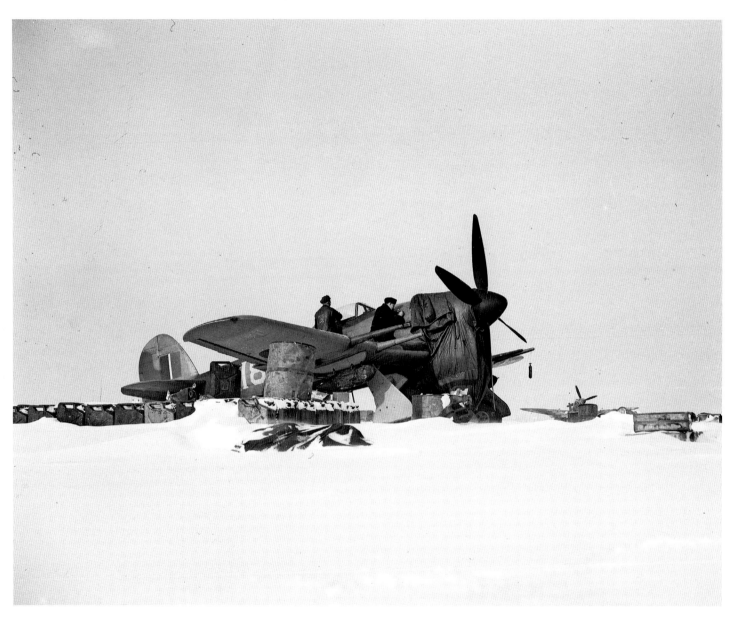

Winter maintenance. Two crewmen begin work on a Typhoon during a bitterly cold day at Eindhoven in February 1945. The fuses for its two 1,000-pound bombs have yet be fitted. DND

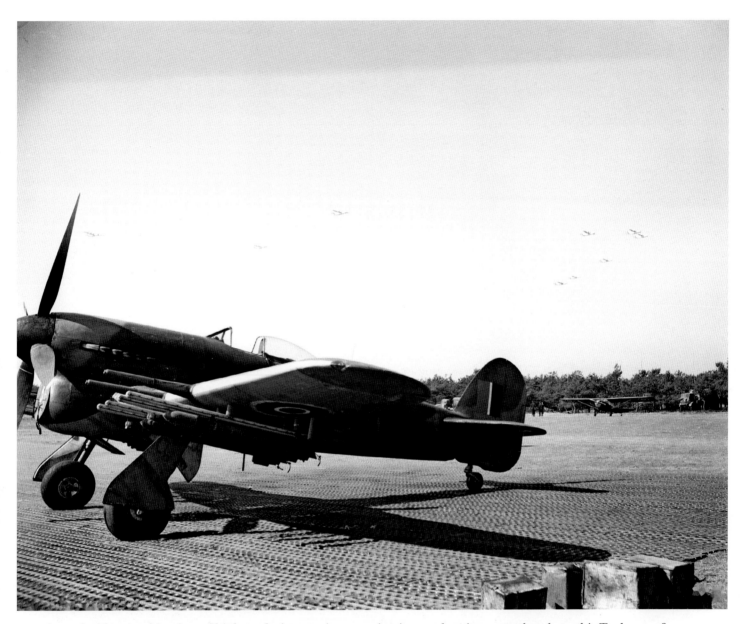

Armed with a combination of high-explosive, semi-armor-piercing, and antipersonnel rockets, this Typhoon of No. 175 Squadron awaits the call to action at its base, B.100 (Goch). In the background, B-24 Liberators can be seen on their way to drop supplies to airborne troops during Operation *Plunder* on March 24, 1945. DND

Mustang IIIs from No. 309 RAF (Polish) fly another escort mission into Germany. On April 9, 1945, this unit scored its last aerial victory of the war, with three pilots sharing in the destruction of an Me 262 near Hamburg. PHIL LISTEMANN

No. 412 Squadron Spitfires undergo outdoor maintenance in March 1945. Serviceability rates for the Spitfire squadrons in the 2nd Tactical Air Force were considered to be very good, with many units achieving the mid- to high-80th percentile. This is a remarkable achievement when most—if not all—maintenance was out in the open, no matter what the weather.

Spitfire Y2-L of No. 442 Squadron RCAF is ready for startup in January 1945. The Spitfire Mk IX's bomb load capability was limited to 1,000 pounds. This example is armed with a single 500-pound bomb. The empty wing racks were capable of holding a single 250-pound bomb each.

The Spitfire Mk XIV was considered one of the best fighters of World War II. Powered by a Rolls Royce Griffon 65 engine developing 2,050 hp that drove a five-bladed airscrew, it had a top speed of 446 mph at 20,000 feet. This Mk XIV RN119 belongs to 441 Squadron RCAF based at B.88 (Heesch) in March 1945.

For aircrews based in England, forward airfields were a godsend. Damaged aircraft could now find the nearest friendly airfield and land. Here, a Spitfire from No. 412 Squadron taxis past B-26G-1, *LA PALOMA*, of the 553rd Bomb Squadron, 386th Bomb Group, at Heesch, Holland, on March 22, 1945.

Two Spitfire Mk XVIs bank for the camera. Assigned to No. 443 Squadron RCAF, they are both equipped with a 45-gallon slipper tank and two wing-mounted bomb racks. The Mk XVI and the Mk VIII were the first Spitfires that finally addressed the issue of its very short range. When introduced in 1945, the new Mk XVI had two additional fuel tanks located behind the pilot, giving the plane 151 gallons of internal fuel. With a 90-gallon slipper tank, that rose to 241 gallons.

The only RAF squadron to be equipped with the new and powerful Spitfire Mk XXI was No. 91 in April 1945. With little or no Luftwaffe activity, the squadron was assigned to search for V-2 rocket sites over Holland. PHIL LISTEMANN

A Spitfire FR Mk XIVE of No. 2 Squadron RAF is seen here in April 1945 at base B.106 (Twente) in Holland.
PHIL LISTEMANN

This H.F. Mk VII
high-altitude version
of the famous Spitfire,
equipped with a
45-gallon drop tank,
belongs to No. 154
Squadron RAF. The
squadron flew its last
escort mission with
the Mk VII in January
1945. PHIL LISTEMANN

The Westland Welkin Mk I is a great example of the Allies' industrial capacity and ability to design and build combat aircraft that would never see action. The Welkin was designed as an extremely high-altitude fighter, capable of reaching 40,000 feet and above. Production of the Welkin Mk I began in 1943, but as the anticipated high-altitude attacks failed to materialize, the Welkin was never issued to a squadron. All examples went straight into storage; in May 1945 there were seventy-six brand-new examples waiting to be scrapped.

Allied fighter-bomber attacks in Northwest Europe were constant and highly effective against transportation targets. This wrecked railway car full of V-1s was found by British troops in early 1945. How many V-1s were destroyed before they reached their launch sites is not known, but it greatly restricted the number that could be launched on any given day.

Marauder Mk III HD581 of No. 39 Squadron RAF runs up for another mission in Italy. In 1945 No. 39 Squadron was the only RAF squadron equipped with the B-26. As part of the Balkan Air Force, No. 39 provided support for Tito's partisan forces in Yugoslavia from December 1944 until the end of the war. PHIL LISTEMANN

Fleet Air Arm Avenger 4H-Q of No. 854 Squadron ends up on its nose after missing the wires in early January 1945. No. 854 Squadron aboard the HMS *Illustrious*—along with No. 820, No. 849, and No. 857 aboard HMS *Illustrious*, HMS *Victorious*, and HMS *Indomitable*—formed the Avenger strike force assigned to the two-phase attack on the Sumatran oil fields starting on January 24. FRANK MITCHELL VIA HOWARD J. MITCHELL

No. 854 Squadron Avengers outbound on the second Sumatran strike that took place on January 29, 1945. The strike group was nearly identical to that of the first raid on the twenty-fourth, with Lt. Cdr. W. J. Mainprice, CO of the *Illustrious'* No. 854 Squadron, leading the way. FRANK MITCHELL VIA HOWARD J. MITCHELL

Smoke from the second Sumatran oil field strike confirms another success on January 29, 1945. As the Fleet Air Arm Avengers head for the rendezvous point after the attack, two Japanese Ki-44s can be seen in the upper left, diving into the attack. When the raid was over, six Avengers ditched near the fleet. These crews were rescued, but unfortunately eleven other Avengers were shot down or forced to land. Avenger crews claimed two Ki-44 "Tojos" shot down. FRANK MITCHELL VIA HOWARD J. MITCHELL

In early March 1945 the British Pacific
Fleet made ready for its part in the
invasion of Okinawa, code-named *Iceberg*.
Redesignated as Task Force 57, its four
carriers were given the job of neutralizing
airfields in the Sakishima Gunto
archipelago. Here, Avengers pound
Hirara Airfield on Miyako in early April.
FRANK MITCHELL VIA HOWARD J. MITCHELL

On April 13, 1945, Avengers from
HMS *Victorious* attacked Shinchiku
Airfield on Taiwan. The bomb
damage is clearly evident. Since Task
Force 57 had no night-bombing
capability, the Japanese could easily
repair their runways overnight.
FRANK MITCHELL VIA HOWARD J. MITCHELL

Carrier operations during World War II were inherently dangerous. Many aircraft and highly trained pilots were lost while trying to land a high-performance aircraft on a narrow, moving steel deck. Here, one Corsair tries to catch a wire aboard the HMS *Illustrious* as another comes up short and is caught in the ship's wake. FRANK MITCHELL VIA HOWARD J. MITCHELL

A Fleet Air Arm Corsair pours on the power for a go-around and torque stalls, slamming into the crash barrier aboard the HMS *Illustrious*. During the Second World War, more naval aircraft were lost due to landing and takeoff accidents than were destroyed in combat. FRANK MITCHELL VIA HOWARD J. MITCHELL

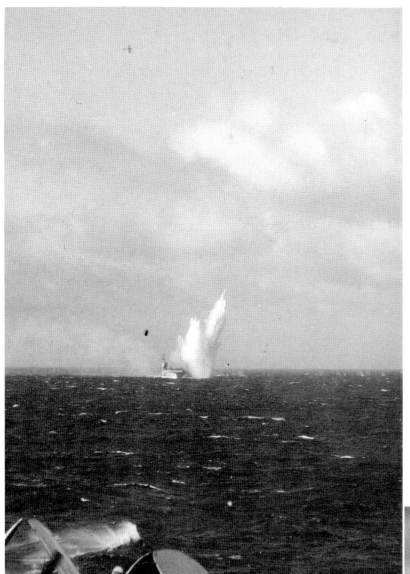

On April 1, 1945, the HMS *Victorious* had a near-miss experience with a determined kamikaze. The starboard wing of the "Jill" or "Zeke" struck the port edge of the flight deck, causing the plane to cartwheel into the sea on the port side. The resulting bomb explosion threw tons of water, petrol, and aircraft fragments onto the flight deck. Directly above the carrier is an aircraft that appears to be a Corsair. FRANK MITCHELL VIA HOWARD J. MITCHELL

A gun-camera still captures the image of a Yokosuka D4Y3 "Judy" as it plunges toward HMS *Illustrious* on April 6, 1945. Diving out of the clouds, the "Judy" was visible for just eleven seconds before it hit the water short of its target. FRANK MITCHELL VIA HOWARD J. MITCHELL

April 12, 1945. British Avengers from Task Force 57 strike targets on Formosa. The strike photo (above) shows bombs exploding around a railway station and two bridges. The post-strike photo (below) clearly shows that the rail bridge is heavily damaged. FRANK MITCHELL VIA HOWARD J. MITCHELL

Seafire IIIs from 801 and 880 Naval Air Squadrons run up their engines on the deck of HMS *Implacable* in early April 1945. To increase their anemic range, these Seafires are equipped with ex–P-40 drop tanks.

The Seafire Mk III was not equipped with hydraulic-powered folding wings. This photo reveals the manpower required to get a Seafire belonging to No. 38 Naval Fighter Wing ready for flight in June 1945.

Mid-1945. A Seafire Mk III warms up its engine aboard HMS *Implacable*. The P-40 drop-tank installation can be clearly seen and doubled the Seafire's range. In the Pacific Theater, Seafires claimed fifteen Zero-sens destroyed during 1945.

A No. 801 Naval Air Squadron Seafire Mk III loses a propeller crashing into HMS *Implacable*'s crash barrier. During the last few months of the war, Seafires began attacking targets on mainland Japan. The results were impressive, with 87 aircraft destroyed on the ground, 3,700 tons of shipping sunk, and 24,700 tons damaged.

On May 5, 1945, a Zero-sen carrying a 250-kilogram bomb struck HMS *Formidable*. The explosion was devastating, with eleven aircraft destroyed, eight sailors killed, and fifty-one wounded. The *Formidable*, however, was saved by its armored deck. Speed was reduced to eighteen knots, and the carrier was out of action for just five hours.

A Fairey Barracuda Mk II poses for an aircraft recognition photograph. Introduced in 1943, the Barracuda was intended to replace the Swordfish and Albacore and served until the end of the war. Like the Swordfish and Albacore, the Barracuda was tasked with several different requirements: dive-bomber, torpedo bomber, and antisubmarine aircraft roles. These demands led to the adaptation of a high wing with windows beneath.

A Fairey Barracuda with its Youngman dive-bombing flaps deployed. The Barracuda was considered very stable in a dive, but during its early service life it suffered a high rate of unexplained fatal crashes. In 1945 the crashes were traced to small leaks in the aircraft's hydraulic system, specifically around the pilot's pressure gauge. Unsuspecting pilots were being sprayed by hydraulic fluid containing ether, rendering them unconscious. For experienced pilots, Fleet Air Arm lieutenant commander Bertie Vigrass said the Barracuda was "not difficult to fly, but it was easy to mishandle."

Avenger overboard. During operations against Sakishima in 1945, this Avenger suffered engine failure shortly after taking off from HMS *Smiter*. The crew can be seen scrambling into the water.

A Firefly Mk 1 of No. 1770 NAS unfolds its wings in preparation for the Sumatra oil refinery raid on January 24, 1945. During this mission, the Firefly scored its first air-to-air kill. The victim was a Ki-43 "Oscar." VIA ANDREW THOMAS

Corsair IIs and Barracuda Mk IIs crowd the front deck of HMS *Illustrious* on January 24, 1945. Corsair 7R/JT433, flown by Lt. Percy Cole of No. 1833 Squadron, was credited with a Ki-45 "Nick" shot down on that day.
VIA ANDREW THOMAS

When the British Pacific Fleet moved into the Pacific to join their American cousins, they had to adopt new markings. Here, a Corsair Mk II from No. 1834 NAS clearly shows the new white bars and white center circle roundels, designed to be similar to the markings used by the U.S. Navy. VIA ANDREW THOMAS

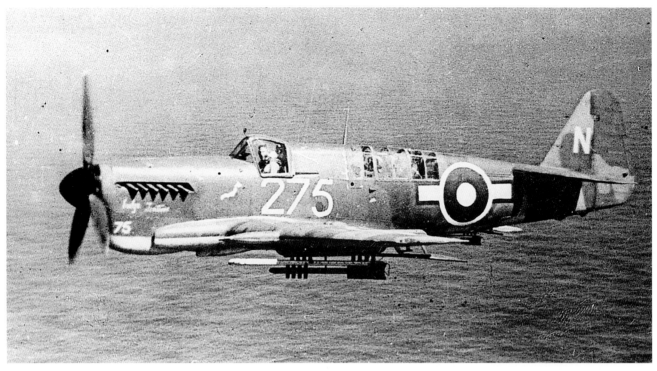

A Firefly from No. 1771 NAS from HMS *Implacable* heads for a target in Japan in July 1945. At this stage of the war, rocket-armed Fireflies were flying "Ramrod" missions—offensive fighter sweeps over Japan. VIA ANDREW THOMAS

When the British Pacific Fleet began operations, it was equipped with thirty-eight Grumman Hellcats with No. 1839 and No. 1844 NAS aboard HMS *Indomitable*. Missing the wires, Hellcat 5A/JX758 of No. 1839 NAS goes over the side of the *Indomitable* on February 27, 1945. VIA ANDREW THOMAS

42 AIR COMBAT 1945

The battle against German U-boats continued right up until the last day of the war. Here, a Fairey Swordfish of No. 816 Squadron warms up aboard HMS *Tracker* for an antisubmarine sweep in early 1945. Each aircraft is armed with eight rocket projectiles.

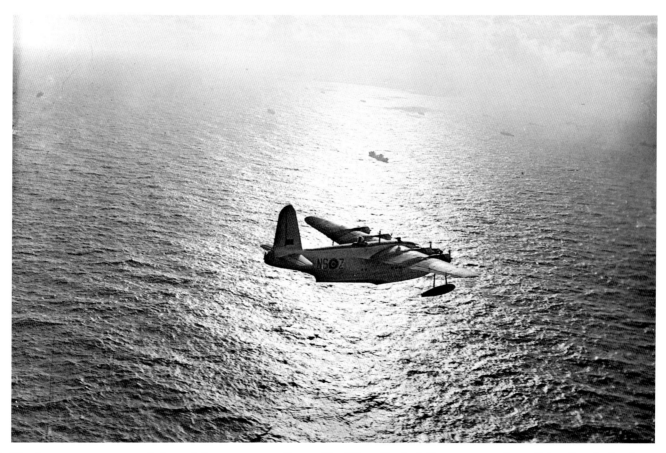

The last convoy escort mission of the war was performed by Wing Cmdr. J. Barrett, seen here flying Sunderland NS-Z in June 1945. The mission occurred four weeks after the German surrender. DND

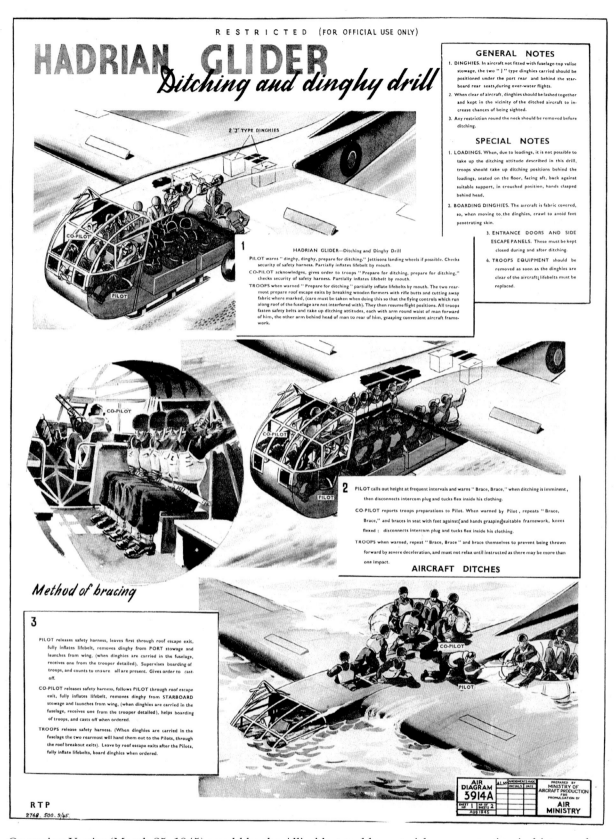

Operation Varsity (March 25, 1945) would be the Allies' last and largest airborne operation in history, when more than 900 Waco CG-4As helped transport over 16,000 air- and glider-borne troops. Named Hadrian by the British, the Waco was constructed from metal, wood, and fabric and capable of carrying two pilots and thirteen combat-ready troops. Flying into combat in a fully loaded glider was extremely hazardous, and accidents were common. In this poster, issued by the Ministry of Aircraft Production, the "Ditching and Dinghy Drill" is explained in detail. Sadly, if the glider had to ditch in the open sea, the rate of survival was almost zero.

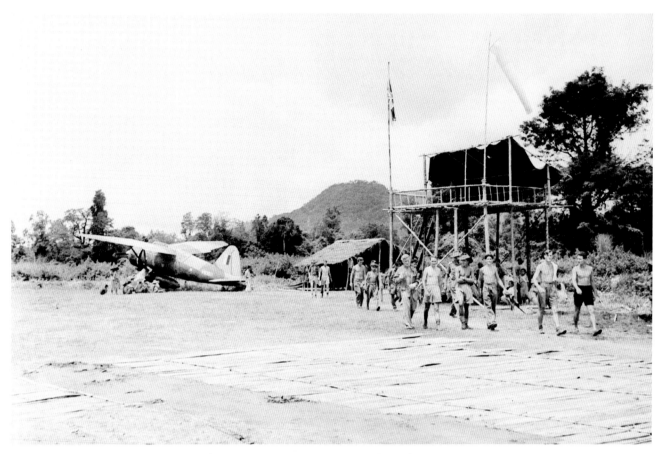

A Lysander of C Flight from No. 357 Squadron RAF is seen here in Burma in 1945. C Flight was formed to operate Lysanders, with the task of picking up agents and supplying Force 136 behind enemy lines. PHIL LISTEMANN

A Liberator Mk III of No. 355 Squadron RAF. Formed as a heavy-bomber unit in August 1943, No. 355 Squadron was an integral part of the Allies' strategic air campaign against the Japanese in Burma. PHIL LISTEMANN

No. 2 Squadron RAAF was the only unit to fly the fabled B-25 Mitchell during World War II. The Australians received their first B-25s, seen here in 1945, as surplus from the Dutch, but later obtained direct Lend-Lease aircraft from the United States. PHIL LISTEMANN

By 1945 all RAF Spitfire squadrons in the Far East were equipped with the Mk VIII. Here, armorers of No. 607 Squadron manhandle a 500-pound bomb for another ground-attack mission. PHIL LISTEMANN

Shark-mouthed Spitfire Mk VIIIs of No. 457 Squadron RAAF are seen here at Morotai. During the summer of 1945, No. 457 flew in support of ground troops fighting the remaining Japanese forces in New Guinea and Timor.

No. 81 Squadron RAF of the FEAF was equipped with P-47D Thunderbolts in the summer of 1945, but was too late to see any action. It did, however, provide air-support missions for Dutch forces during the Indonesian War of Independence in October 1945. PHIL LISTEMANN

The Hawker Tempest Mk V was arguably the best medium- to low-altitude fighter of the war. Compared to the Griffon–powered Spitfire Mk XIV, the Tempest was 20 mph faster between sea level and 10,000 feet; above 10,000 feet they were roughly equal, but when the Spitfire XIV reached 22,000 feet, it was 30–40 mph faster. Seven squadrons served with the 2nd Tactical Air Force.

The de Havilland Vampire Mk 1 was Britain's second jet fighter. The first production Mk 1 flew on April 20, 1945. Powered by a single de Havilland Goblin II turbojet, the new Vampire completely outclassed the Spitfire Mk XIV, 140 mph faster at ground level.

Aircraft recognition by both antiaircraft crews and pilots during World War II was not very good. In order to keep gunners from mistaking the Meteor for an Me 262, the British painted their Meteors completely white while serving on the Continent. TONY BUTLER COLLECTION

Meteor Mk III EE239 of No. 616 Squadron RAF takes off over a mobile Chance light. In February No. 616 Squadron received its first Derwent–powered Meteor III. Engine thrust went from 1,700 pounds to 2,000 pounds, giving the Meteor a top speed of 493 mph at 30,000 feet and 453 mph at sea level. TONY BUTLER COLLECTION

Armorers load 25-pound RPs onto Mosquito FB.VI PZ438 at Banff in February 1945. This aircraft would be lost due to flak while flying over Alesund, Norway, on March 17, 1945. PHIL LISTEMANN

A Mosquito FB.VI of No. 143 Squadron, the Banff Strike Wing, is seen here on a chilly day in early 1945. On May 4, the Banff Strike Wing flew their last large-scale shipping strike of the war. One merchant ship was sunk and two damaged, with a loss of one Mosquito and four escorting Mustangs. PHIL LISTEMANN

Farnborough, November 1946. This photograph represents the state of the art in piston-engine combat aircraft technology and the transition into the jet age. Here, some of the best piston-engine fighters and bombers from both the Luftwaffe and RAF sit side by side. Back row, left to right: a Ju 290, a Ju 52/3, a Ju 352, an Fw 200, and a Do 217. A Ju 88 Mistel combination can just be seen right at the back. Second row, left to right: an Si 204, a Ju 88G, an Fi 103–manned V-1, a Ju 188, a Ju 388, an He 219, and an Fw 189. Third row, left to right: an Me 410, a Bf 110G, a Do 335B-12 trainer, a Ta 152, an Fw 190A, a Bf 109G, an Fi 156 Storch, an Ar 234, and an Me 262. Final row, left to right: a Supermarine Spiteful, a Martin-Baker MB 5, a Blackburn Firebrand, a Bristol Brigand, a Fairey Firefly, a Fairey Spearfish, a Meteor, and a couple of late-mark Tempest tails.

August 1945, Kassel Airfield, Germany. Two Americans examine the fuselage of a Messerschmitt Me 263/Junkers Ju 248. The Me 263 improved on the original Me 163 rocket fighter with a larger and better-shaped body, a new engine, and retractable landing gear. Production of the new Me 263 was shifted to Junkers and improved even more with automatic slats, a bubble hood, and cut-down rear fuselage; however, the Me 263/Ju 248 never saw action. Beside this Me 263 are several Fieseler Fi 103 piloted missiles; two He 162 jet fighters are in the background.

By war's end, thousands of unserviceable Luftwaffe aircraft littered captured airfields across Germany. Pilot Officer Eric Slater of 402 Squadron is seen here sitting on a broken Fw 190F at Wunstorf Airfield in May 1945. Specialized for close-support, the Fw 190F was heavily armored, with the lower-engine cowling and wheel covers made of 6mm armor plate. In addition, 6mm plates were applied to the underside of the fuselage, for a total armor weight of 800 pounds. CANADIAN WARPLANE HERITAGE MUSEUM

This Fw 190F was one of the many ground-attack versions of the famous Focke-Wulf fighters built during the war. This example was found intact at Wunstorf Airfield in Germany. The Fw 190F was equipped with a single belly-mounted ETC 501 bomb rack and two ETC 50 bomb racks per wing. CANADIAN WARPLANE HERITAGE MUSEUM

The Henschel Hs 162 was the standard German Army cooperation aircraft at the beginning of the war. By 1942 they were phased out of service, but would return in the role of night harassment. In January 1945 *Nachtschlachtgruppen* NSGr7, based in the Balkans, was equipped with both the Hs 162 and the Italian CR.42LW. This example was abandoned at Wunstorf Airfield. CANADIAN WARPLANE HERITAGE MUSEUM

Pilot Officer Eric Slater of 402 Squadron lounges on the wing of a damaged late-model Bf 109G or K at Wunstorf in May 1945. As of April 9, 1945, the *Luftwaffenkommando West* had just 178 serviceable Bf 109s on strength.

Gun-camera images taken in early 1945 from an unidentified U.S. Eighth Air Force P-47 or P-51 clearly show a lucky German pilot jumping for his life from his damaged Fw 190. Smoke can be seen streaming from the aircraft in the right of the center photograph.

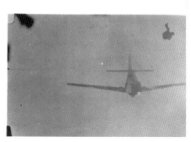

A burnt-out Fw 190D-9, W.Nr. 210980, at an airfield in Germany in 1945. The Fw 190D was nicknamed "Dora" and was Germany's best piston-engine fighter of the war. In April 1945, *Jagdgeschwader 6* received 150 brand-new Fw 190D-9s; however, the severe lack of fuel limited the unit to flying standing patrols of four aircraft at a time. Approximately 700 Fw 190Ds were completed before the end of the war.

This burnt-out Fw 190 appears to be a ground-attack version of the famous "Butcher Bird." The lack of an outboard 20mm cannon and the breech of the inboard gun can be seen clearly in the burnt-out area of the wing root. This aircraft was most likely a late model F, as evidenced by the 13mm Rheinmetall MG 131 sticking up in the air. The Fw 190F-8 was armed with two 13mm machine guns and two 20mm cannon. NATIONAL MUSEUM OF THE USAF

The Focke-Wulf Fw 190G-1 was one of several ground-attack versions of the Fw 190 produced during the war. The Fw 190G-1 could carry a 550-pound or 1,100-pound bomb on the centerline rack and two underwing drop tanks on the VTr-Ju 87 racks, as seen here. NATIONAL MUSEUM OF THE USAF

The Henschel Hs 129 was the only aircraft in World War II to be designed as a tank killer. Seen here with No. 1426 Flight RAF in 1945, this B-1 example (W.Nr. 0296) was shipped in parts from North Africa and reassembled. Flown in September 1944, it was plagued with constant engine problems and finally grounded sometime in January 1945. The Henschel Hs 129 served until the end of the war with the Luftwaffe's *10.(Pz)/SG 9*, the last unit to do so.

Focke Wulf 190D-9 W.Nr. 210079 is seen here at R.A.E. Farnborough in 1945. Captured in Belgium, it was shipped to Britain for examination. This airframe was used by British Air Intelligence for the first full-color cutaway air diagram of an Fw 190D.

A captured Fw 190D-9 "Dora." Arguably the Luftwaffe's best single-seat, piston-engine fighter of the war, it entered service in late summer 1944 with *III/JG 54*. Its first task was to provide fighter cover for Me 262 jet fighters during takeoff and landing, when they were most vulnerable. NATIONAL MUSEUM OF THE USAF

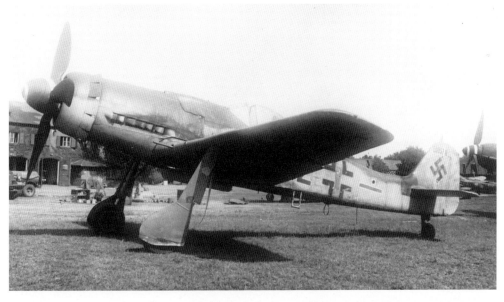

This Fw 190D-9, *Black 12*, W.Nr. 50070, belonged to *II/JG 6*. To avoid capture by the Soviets, it was one of four D-9s flown west by German pilots to Fürth, near Nürnberg. There, they were surrendered to elements of the U.S. 10th Photo Reconnaissance Group on May 8, 1945. NATIONAL MUSEUM OF THE USAF

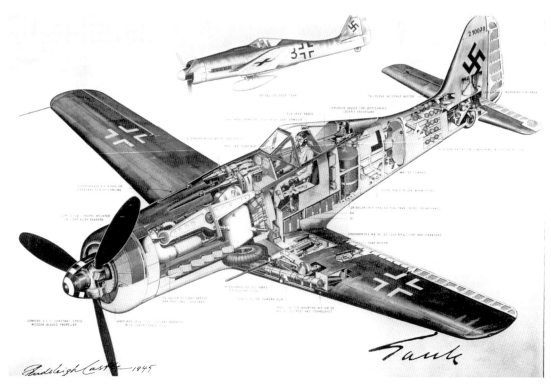

Peter Castle produced this exceptional cutaway air diagram of the Fw 190D-9 for distribution in 1945. Fortunately, the war in Europe ended before distribution began. The aircraft used for this highly detailed drawing was Fw 190D-9 W.Nr.210079, captured in Belgium in 1945. Under interrogation after the war, Kurt Tank, designer of the Fw 190D-9, was so impressed by Castle's drawing that he signed it (see the bottom right).

Often identified as a *Bodenplatte* victim, this Fw 190D-9 was in fact found postwar at Frankfurt's Rhein-Main Airfield. This aircraft, formerly belonging to the *Stabsschwarm JG 4*, force-landed (note the shattered propeller blades), coming to grief in the last few days of the war.

A Junkers Ju 88G-1 night fighter equipped with SN-2 airborne radar. The Ju 88G model was arguably the best night fighter of the war and served to the end. With excellent range and adequate space for extra equipment, it was well armed and flown by many of Germany's top night-fighter aces. In January 1945 the *Nachtjagd* had 372 serviceable Ju 88G night fighters on strength. It was an impressive number, but the *Nachtjagd* was a force facing extinction. By April there were just sixty-five Ju 88G night fighters serviceable for operations.

The Arado Ar 234 was one of the more remarkable aircraft of World War II. As the world's first purpose-built jet bomber, it handled well at all speeds, but became sluggish with a full bomb load. This Ar 234B-2 of *KG 76* is equipped with bomb racks under the engine nacelles, giving it a maximum load of 3,300 pounds. By April 1945, just five Ar 234s were serviceable.

The vast majority of Me 262s produced during the final months of the war never saw combat. As the Allies closed in, many of the aircraft were reduced to broken hulks. The Germans immobilized a large number by strapping an explosive charge in the nose, thus preventing the Allies from using the jets. NATIONAL MUSEUM OF THE USAF

A captured Me 262A-1a/U4 taken at Lager Lechfeld in early June 1945. This example is armed with a powerful 50mm Mauser MK 214 cannon. Just two Me 262s were modified to carry this weapon and tested in March/April 1945. NATIONAL MUSEUM OF THE USAF

This shot shows the unguided R4M rockets ("M" stands for *Minenkopf,* German for "explosive head") mounted on an Me 262A-1a of *JG 7.* On April 20, 1945, six Me 262s from *JV-44* shot down three B-26 Marauders from the 323rd Bomb Group, using cannon and rocket fire. NATIONAL MUSEUM OF THE USAF

Completed Me 262s roll off the production line at the Laupheim factory, south of Ulm. This heavily camouflaged factory continued to produce large numbers of Me 262s during the early months of 1945. NATIONAL MUSEUM OF THE USAF

Me 262B-1a/U1 (W.Nr. 111980, *Red 12*) of *Lt.* Herbert Altner of *10./NJG 11* was captured at Reinfeld airfield in May 1940. The night-fighter version was equipped with FuG 218 Neptun V radar and two 300-liter drop tanks.
NATIONAL MUSEUM OF THE USAF

The remains of an Me 262A-1a destroyed by Allied airpower. Attacked in the air and on the ground, the small force of Me 262s available to the Luftwaffe had no impact on the air war in the final months of hostilities.
NATIONAL MUSEUM OF THE USAF

The front end of Me 262A-1a *White 7* from *III/JG 7*. This aircraft was surrendered at Fassberg on May 8, 1945, by *Uffz.* Gunther Engler. The Me 262 was well armed, with four Rheinmetall-Borsig 30mm Mk 108 cannon and 360 rounds of ammunition. One short burst was more than enough to destroy a four-engine heavy bomber. 1000AIRCRAFT.COM

Yellow 17 of *III/JG 7*, seen here beside *White 7*, was also surrendered on May 8, 1945, by *Lt.* Hans Dorn. *JG 7* was the most prolific operator of the Me 262, receiving more Me 262s—and pilots—than any other *Geschwader*.
1000AIRCRAFT.COM

Another view of *Yellow 17*. On May 8, 1945, several *JG 7* pilots flew their aircraft from Prague back into Germany. It was also the day on which the last aerial victory by an Me 262 was scored: *Oberleutnant* Stehle of *JG 7* was credited with two Soviet Yak-9s destroyed over the Erz Mountain range. 1000AIRCRAFT.COM

A well-camouflaged Heinkel He 177A-5 is seen somewhere in Germany 1945. Starved of fuel by August 1944, the Luftwaffe was forced to ground the majority of its He 177s. When production of the He 177 ceased, 565 examples of the A-5 had been built. In January 1945 *II/KG 100* listed thirty-two as serviceable. 1000AIRCRAFT.COM

Heavily camouflaged He 177s are strafed by marauding P-51s. By 1945 an He 177 caught on the ground was not a high-value target. Lack of fuel had all but grounded the entire He 177 fleet—far too many Allied pilots were shot down while attacking these fuel-starved bombers.

Aided by a mechanic, an Me 163 pilot readies himself for another flight in the volatile rocket fighter. To safeguard against any leaks of the toxic fuel mixture, the pilot was forced to wear a one-piece protective suit and gloves. The Me 163's combat history was short and unimpressive. It entered service in May 1944 with the *I/JG 400*, the world's first rocket-fighter unit, which had just eight victories by the end of the year. By the opening weeks of 1945, the situation went from bad to worse. Lack of fuel curtailed operations, with just two victories claimed. By May 1945 *I/JG 400* claimed just ten enemy aircraft shot down.

An Me 163B-1a roars to full power (the shock diamonds in the rocket exhaust can be clearly seen). Of all Me 163 losses, 80 percent were the result of accidents during takeoff and landing. By May 1945 the Komets of *JG 400* claimed just sixteen Allied aircraft destroyed. NATIONAL MUSEUM OF THE USAF

Roaming Allied fighters destroyed an undetermined number of Luftwaffe night fighters during daylight hours. Although the Allies were aware of the Heinkel He 219, they had no oblique photos of the aircraft. This rather blurred gun-camera image caused considerable interest in early 1945. NATIONAL MUSEUM OF THE USAF

A three-view aircraft recognition profile of the He 219 *Uhu* produced by A.I. 2 (G) (Air Intelligence 2 (G)). The He 219 was a very advanced night-fighter design with a number of novel features, including ejector seats, an all-around canopy, and interchangeable weapon packs. NATIONAL MUSEUM OF THE USAF

A captured Junkers Ju 290A-7 long-range maritime reconnaissance bomber. The A-7 version featured an enlarged nose with a handheld 20mm MG 151 cannon. About five Ju 290A-7s were built; this example, coded A3+HB, served with *KG 200*. NATIONAL MUSEUM OF THE USAF

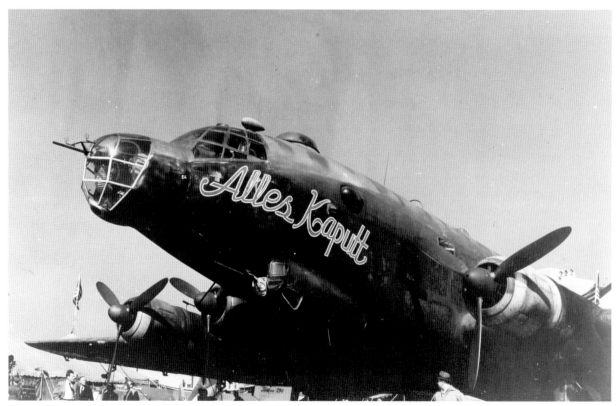

By May 1945 German airfields were littered with hundreds of abandoned and wrecked aircraft. This Bf 109 is a late-model G-10 or K-4 version with the *Erla* canopy. The K-4 was the last operational version of the famous Messerschmitt fighter to enter service. It was powered by the DB 605 ASCM/DCM with MW 50 (methanol) injection, boosting takeoff power from 1,550 hp to 2,000 hp; its top speed was 452 mph at 19,685 feet. NATIONAL MUSEUM OF THE USAF

A Bf 110G-4b/R3 on display at an exhibition of captured enemy aircraft at Farnborough in October 1945. Both the Bf 110 and the Ju 88 were the core types used by the *Nachtjagd* in the defense of Germany. The Bf 110G-4b/R3 was equipped with both SN-2 and FuG 212 radar systems and long-range fuel tanks. Ironically, there were just as many Bf 110 night fighters in service at the end of the war as there were at the beginning.

Using existing war-weary G-2/4/6 airframes, the G-12 was a dedicated two-seat trainer version of the "Gustav" series. A total of 494 G-12s were modified by Blohm & Voss between September 1943 and December 1944. By January 1945 lack of fuel all but ended pilot training in Germany, except for those destined to fly the Me 262. The Me 262 training unit *III/EJG 2* was equipped with a dozen late-model Bf 109Gs and Ks, plus four or five Bf 109G-12s or Fw 190S two-seaters. NATIONAL MUSEUM OF THE USAF

A wrecked Bf 109G is seen here in Germany 1945. The aircraft has a green "Defense of the Reich" band around the rear fuselage. By 1945 these colored identification markings gradually disappeared as the Reich crashed into chaos and confusion. An incredible total of 24,000 Bf 109s were built during the war. NATIONAL MUSEUM OF THE USAF

Junkers Ju 87 D-5 V8+JB of *NSGr. I—Nord* at Wunstorf Airfield in April/May 1945. The white band around the cowling indicates "northern" planes of the Luftwaffe. *NSGr. I* was a specialized night-bombing unit (note the exhaust flame damper) used against both American and British forces. By February 1945 *NSGr. I* had been divided in two: *NSGr. I—Nord* and *NSGr. I—Sud.* Retreating to the north, *NSGr. I* finally surrendered at Husum with just one Ju 87D-5 left. 1000AIRCRAFT.COM

A Ju 88G-10 twined with an Fw 190A-8 to form a Mistel pilotless missile aircraft. One of the last Mistel combinations flown in the final few weeks of the war, it consisted of a Ta 152H/Ju 88G-7. NATIONAL MUSEUM OF THE USAF

American troops captured Dornier's Oberpfaffenhofen factory in April 1945. There they found nine Do 335A-1s, four A-4s, and a pair of A-12s in final assembly. NATIONAL MUSEUM OF THE USAF

The Do 335A-10 two-seat trainer prototype. The Do 335 was the most unconventional piston-engine fighter developed by the Germans during the war, but its tractor-pusher configuration proved successful, with a maximum speed of 474 mph at 21,325 feet. NATIONAL MUSEUM OF THE USAF

A captured Blohm & Voss Bv 222C-012 Wiking seen here at Trondheim, Norway, in May 1945. This version was powered by six Jumo 207c diesel engines. Three different versions of the monster Bv 222 were captured by the Allies and tested by both British and U.S. pilots. NATIONAL MUSEUM OF THE USAF

The aft defensive armament of the Ju 188 consisted of a dorsal 13mm MG 131 electro-hydraulically operated EDL 131/1D turret and one handheld 13mm MG 131 machine gun. In its last combat mission of the war, the Ju 188 did not fare well. On April 25, 1945, a mixed formation of six Ju 188A-17s from *6/KG 26s* and twelve Ju 88s from *7/KG 27* headed for the Scottish coast in search of shipping. Unfortunately, the formation was spotted by forty-five Mosquitos of the Banff Strike Wing returning at dusk from an uneventful patrol to Kattegat. In the ensuring fight, nine Junkers were shot down with no loss to the strike wing.

The torpedo version of the Junkers Ju 188. This Ju 188E-2 was equipped with underwing racks capable of carrying two 1,763-pound LT-1B or 1,686-pound LT F5b torpedoes. It was also equipped with the FuG 200 Hohenweil antiship radar. FuG 200–equipped Ju 188s based in Norway and Denmark saw sporadic service from January to April 1945. NATIONAL MUSEUM OF THE USAF

This cutaway drawing by artist R. Redmill was produced by A.I. 2 (G) in late 1945. By the time this drawing was issued, the Me 163 had all but ceased operations. NATIONAL MUSEUM OF THE USAF

The cockpit and flight instrument panel of the Junkers Ju 388L-1 W.Nr. 560049. This example was captured in May 1945 at Merseberg and shipped back to the United States for testing. Vision from the cockpit was described in a 1945 USAF Evaluation Report as "excellent downward and forward, although somewhat restricted laterally and to the rear." NATIONAL MUSEUM OF THE USAF

Ar 234 Arado Bu.No 121445, seen here at Patuxent River in 1946, was not flown due to lack of spares. This B-2 version is equipped with two bomb racks under each engine nacelle, giving it a bomb load capability of 3,300 pounds.

A captured Arado Ar 234B-2 undergoing engine maintenance. The Ar 234 used a similar engine installation to the Me 262 fighter, with long, narrow nacelles slung below the inboard part of the wing. Like the Me 262, the Ar 234 was powered by the Jumo OO4B *Orkan* turbojet and ran on J2 fuel. NATIONAL MUSEUM OF THE USAF

This Junkers Ju 287 V1 captured by the Allies was truly a "Frankenstein" bomber. Using the fuselage of an He 177, a tail unit from a Ju 388, and a nose wheel from a B-24, it was powered by four Jumo 004B-1 turbojets. Flight-testing of the Ju 287 with forward-swept wings continued well into 1945. NATIONAL MUSEUM OF THE USAF

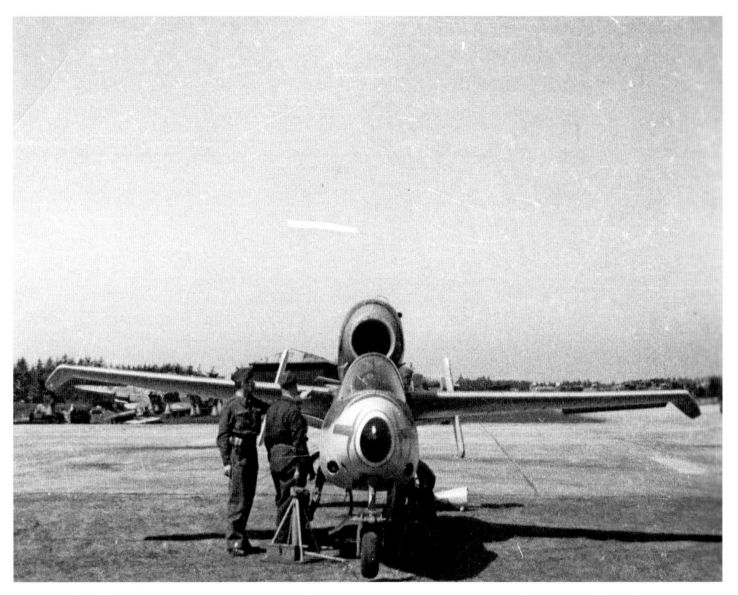

An He 162A-2 of *3./Jagdgeschwader 1* at Leck/Holstein is examined by two British soldiers in May 1945. World-renowned British test pilot Capt. Eric Brown described the He 162 as an "effective gun platform," capable of running rings around the Gloster Meteor Mk III. NATIONAL MUSEUM OF THE USAF

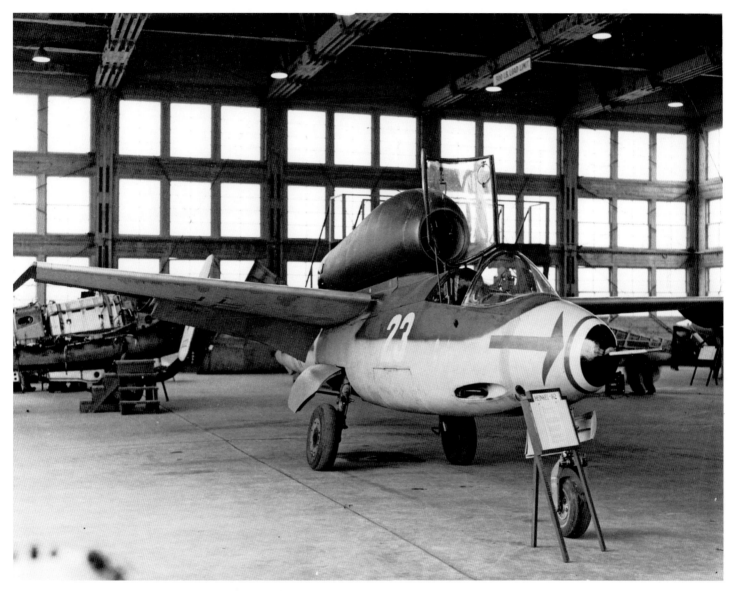

This He 162A-2 was acquired at Leck and one of three examples taken to the United States for tests and evaluation. The airframe is now in the National Air and Space Museum's collection. NATIONAL MUSEUM OF THE USAF

A line of Bf 110G-2s at Solar Aerodrome, Stavanger, Norway, just after VE-Day. These aircraft belong to *IV/ZG 26*, formed in late 1944. The aircraft have had their rudders removed (see second and third in line) in order to immobilize them.

In May 1944 the Allies agreed to reequip the Italian Co-Belligerent Air Force with more modern aircraft. By December 1944, *20° Gruppo* of the *51° Stormo* was equipped with Spitfire Mk Vs. In 1945 the Mk Vs were replaced by newer Mk IXs, as seen here. On May 5 Spitfires of *20° Gruppo* flew the last *Regia Aeronautica* operation of the war. GIORGIO APOSTOLO

A Bf 109G-6, *Yellow 10*, of *2° Gruppo* of the *Aeronautica Repubblicana* (Republican Air Force, ANR) warms up for another flight. At the beginning of January 1945, *2° Gruppo* was equipped with twenty serviceable Bf 109s, twelve of which were G-6s. GIORGIO APOSTOLO

A well-camouflaged Bf 109G-10/AS of the *I° Gruppo* warms up for one of its final operations in March 1945. On April 19 *I° Gruppo* flew its last fighter mission of the war and claimed one B-24 destroyed. GIORGIO APOSTOLO

In the second half of 1944, the fighter groups of the ANR were equipped with the latest versions of the Bf 109, a mixed bag of G-4, G-6, G-10, G-12, and G-14 models. This Bf 109G-10/AS of the *I° Gruppo* is manhandled during maintenance at Malpensa in February 1945. GIORGIO APOSTOLO

Bf 109G-19/AS W.Nr.491333, *2ª Squadriglia, 2° Gruppo*, taxis out for another mission at Lonate Pozzolo. On April 19 this aircraft was damaged during combat in which the unit scored its last victory of the war. GIORGIO APOSTOLO

Bf 109G-10/AS *Black 11* prepares for combat at Aviano in 1945. This aircraft belonged to *2ª Squadriglia, 2° Gruppo*, piloted by S. M. Baldi; he was shot down and bailed out on April 2. GIORGIO APOSTOLO

Two S.M. 79bis torpedo bombers. The one closest to the camera has the code B1-09, serial number MM22285, and belongs to *Gruppo "Buscaglia"* of the ANR. These aircraft had the new black camouflage scheme for night operations. *Gruppo "Buscaglia"* was dissolved in late 1944 and renamed *"Faggioni."* On January 5, 1945, two *"Faggioni"* S.M. 79s sank a 5,000-ton ship in the Adriatic during the group's last operation of the war. GIORGIO APOSTOLO

A Fiat G.55 *Serie I* of the *2° Gruppo* ANR in July 1944. The G.55 was the best Italian fighter of the war. Better than the Bf 109G and Fw 190A, it was fast, well armed, and capable of taking on the greatest the Allies had to offer. Fortunately for the Allies, the G.55 did not see action in 1945; however, it was tested as a torpedo bomber. In January 1945 a single G.55S equipped with a torpedo was deemed suitable for operations, but the war ended before any more of these aircraft were built. GIORGIO APOSTOLO

1° Stormo of the RA Co-Belligerent Air Force received a number of well-used ex–RAF Baltimore IVs and Vs in July 1944. As part of the RAF's Balkan Air Force, the *1° Stormo* flew continuous operations over Yugoslavia from 1944 until the end of the war. On May 4 *1° Stormo* flew its last mission of the war. GIORGIO APOSTOLO

In June 1944 *12° Gruppo* and *4° Stormo* of the RA Co-Belligerent Air Force gave up their old MC.205Vs for the Bell P-39Qs Airacobras seen in the background. The P-39s flew missions against German forces over Yugoslavia in escort, dive-bombing, and strafing attacks until May 1945. At the end of hostilities, the RA had sixty operational P-39Qs.
GIORGIO APOSTOLO

The Macchi MC.205V *Veltro* would soldier on with the RA Co-Belligerent Air Force until the end of the war. Forced to scour the battlefields of Africa, Sicily, Sardinia, and southern Italy for spare parts, ground crews struggled to keep MC.205s fit for combat. Here, MC.205Vs of the *1° Gruppo* undergo engine maintenance in the spring of 1944. On May 8, 1945, the RA's Order of Battle listed thirty MC.205Vs, nineteen of which were operational.
GIORGIO APOSTOLO

A Z.1007 of *88° Gruppo* in 1945. Tasked with flying supplies to Yugoslavian partisans, the Z.1007 operated continuously from 1943 until the end of hostilities. The last drop was carried out on April 26, 1945. GIORGIO APOSTOLO

The SM.79bis served in both the RA in the south and the ANR in the north during 1945. With the ANR it functioned as a torpedo bomber, and with the RA it was used as a transport. This SM.79bis belongs to the *3° Stormo, 2° Gruppo*, at Galatina in 1945.

German flak defenses remained deadly right up until the end of the war. This B-17 LG-W, serial number 4231333, of the 91st Bomb Group is torn apart by a direct hit on April 10, 1945. This B-17 may have been destroyed by the Luftwaffe's new projectile with a contact and timed fuse (*Dopplezunder*). During combat trials on April 9, heavy flak batteries using the new shell brought down thirteen bombers at a cost of just 370 rounds per shoot-down.

Two B-24s of the 409th Squadron, 93rd Bomb Group, plow through heavy flak over Augsburg on March 1, 1945. Only one B-24 was damaged beyond repair due to flak.

On April 10, 1945, the 648 B-24s and B-17s of the Fifteenth Air Force flew in support of Allied ground troops near Lugo, Italy. After dropping fragmentation bombs on enemy artillery, installations, and troop concentrations, B-24L-10-FO, serial number 44-49710, of the 77th Bombardment Squadron, 464th Bomb Group, was shot down by flak. There was only one survivor.

A B-26 Marauder of the 334th Bomb Group, 497th Bomb Squadron, receives a direct flak hit over Germany in March 1945. Between April 20, 1944, and April 20, 1945, the 397th completed 239 combat operations.

The "Mighty Eighth." By January 1945 Allied airpower was overwhelming, both strategically and tactically. For bomber crews just starting their tours, many would never see a German fighter, but flak remained a deadly threat right to the end.

The lead bombardier of the 390th Bomb Group has just released his smoke markers, the signal for the other B-17s in the group to drop their bombs. Started in 1944 and used until the end of the war, the lead bombardier system was standard operating procedure. By 1945 hundreds of well-trained bombardiers never used their Norden bombsights in combat.

A B-26 Marauder from the 453rd Bomb Squadron loses an engine to flak on January 22, 1945. Medium bombers were exposed to more flak than their strategic brothers like the B-17 and B-24, from not only 88mm guns but also 57mm, 37mm, and 20mm medium and light flak cannon.

RIGHT: On April 12, 1945, a Douglas A-26 Invader from the 642nd Bomb Squadron spirals out of control after a direct flak hit. Introduced in September 1944, the A-26 would go on to fly 11,567 sorties with a loss of 67 Invaders to all causes. They were also credited with seven air-to-air kills.

A four-ship element of the 31st Fighter Group begins to roll out prior to diving into action. Wearing the group's distinctive red stripes, each P-51 carries two 75-gallon metal drop tanks. By the end of the war, the 31st was the top-scoring Allied fighter group in the Mediterranean Theater of Operations, with 570.5 confirmed aerial victories.

Like all Allied single-seat fighters, the P-38 Lightning was used extensively as a fighter-bomber. Considered more delicate than the P-47 Thunderbolt in this role, the Lightning was capable of carrying up to 4,000 pounds of bombs. This P-38J is equipped to carry six 500-pound bombs.

In the summer of 1943, the USAAF received more than 100 "reverse Lend-Lease" Bristol Beaufighter Mk VI night fighters. These aircraft were assigned to the 414th, 415th, 416th, and 417th Night Fighter Squadrons based in Italy. By December 1944 the 414th converted to the P-61 Black Widow, and the 415th followed soon after. The 416th received the De Havilland Mosquito NF Mk XIII, while the 417th soldiered on with their war-weary Beaufighters until the end of the war.

A mix of Allied airpower. A well-worn Douglas A-20 shares the mud and water with a number of Spitfires and a solitary P-47 at a forward maintenance unit in northern Italy in the winter of 1945.

Too late to see action, the Lockheed P-80 Shooting Star made it to the front line in Italy just before hostilities ended. Seen here on their Italian airfield, the two YP-80s sent did not encounter any enemy aircraft. A 1945 USAAF report noted that "the [German] Me 262 was superior to the P-80 in acceleration, speed and approximately the same in climb performance."

Splattered with oil, Lt. Edwin King of the 347th Fighter Squadron stands on the wing of his damaged P-47. While escorting a formation of B-25s, King intercepted a small number of Bf 109Gs of the *2° Gruppo* that were attacking the B-25s. The combat resulted in a blown cylinder and a gush of oil over his P-47.

10—SIZE OF BULLET PATTERNS OF B-17 GUNS

DISPERSION OF 12 ROUNDS AIMED AT AN ATTACKING FIGHTER FROM 600 YARDS-BASED ON GROUND FIRING TEST WITH EIGHTH AIR FORCE COMBAT PLANES.

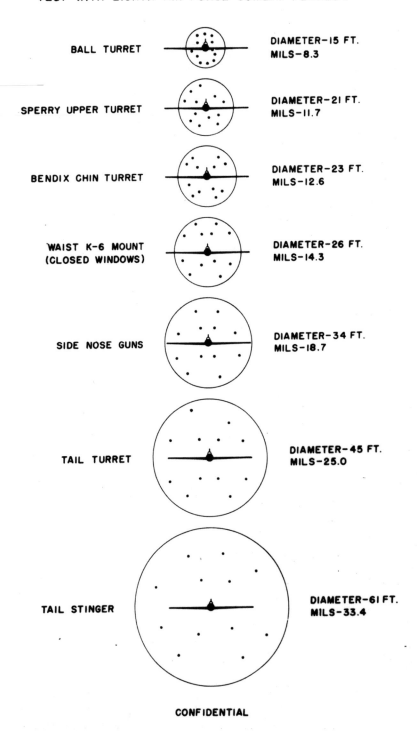

BALL TURRET — DIAMETER-15 FT. MILS-8.3

SPERRY UPPER TURRET — DIAMETER-21 FT. MILS-11.7

BENDIX CHIN TURRET — DIAMETER-23 FT. MILS-12.6

WAIST K-6 MOUNT (CLOSED WINDOWS) — DIAMETER-26 FT. MILS-14.3

SIDE NOSE GUNS — DIAMETER-34 FT. MILS-18.7

TAIL TURRET — DIAMETER-45 FT. MILS-25.0

TAIL STINGER — DIAMETER-61 FT. MILS-33.4

Hitting a fast-moving German fighter with a .50-caliber machine gun from a slow-moving bomber was extremely difficult. These two bullet dispersion charts for both the B-17 and B-24 gun positions graphically illustrate how problematic it was to score a direct hit, even with a stationary ground target.

II—SIZE OF BULLET PATTERNS OF B-24 GUNS

DISPERSION OF 12 ROUNDS AIMED AT AN ATTACKING FIGHTER FROM 600 YARDS—BASED ON GROUND FIRING TEST WITH EIGHTH AIR FORCE COMBAT PLANES.

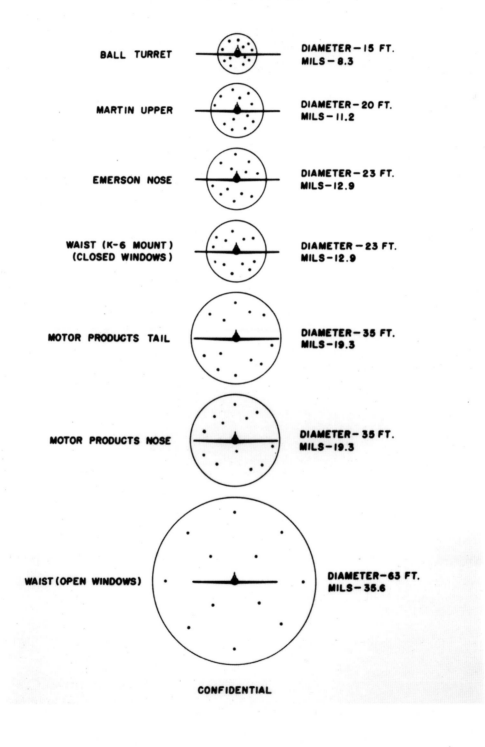

BALL TURRET — DIAMETER—15 FT. MILS—8.3

MARTIN UPPER — DIAMETER—20 FT. MILS—11.2

EMERSON NOSE — DIAMETER—23 FT. MILS—12.9

WAIST (K-6 MOUNT) (CLOSED WINDOWS) — DIAMETER—23 FT. MILS—12.9

MOTOR PRODUCTS TAIL — DIAMETER—35 FT. MILS—19.3

MOTOR PRODUCTS NOSE — DIAMETER—35 FT. MILS—19.3

WAIST (OPEN WINDOWS) — DIAMETER—63 FT. MILS—35.6

The Boeing B-29 Superfortress was the ultimate heavy bomber of World War II. Beginning in the spring of 1944, the B-29 was bombing targets in China and the Pacific. In total, five bomb wings were equipped with the B-29; the most famous was the 509th Composite Group—the atomic bombers.

A Japanese Kawasaki Ki-45 *Toryu* "Nick" twin-engine fighter plunges through a formation of B-29s from the 6th Bomb Squadron, 29th Bomb Group. The top B-29 has been damaged and is beginning to break formation.

The B-29's General Electric remote computer-aided turret gun system was the most advanced of the war. For gunners, this sophisticated aiming system was capable of automatically correcting for range, altitude, airspeed, and temperature. This photo shows the rear ventral turret.

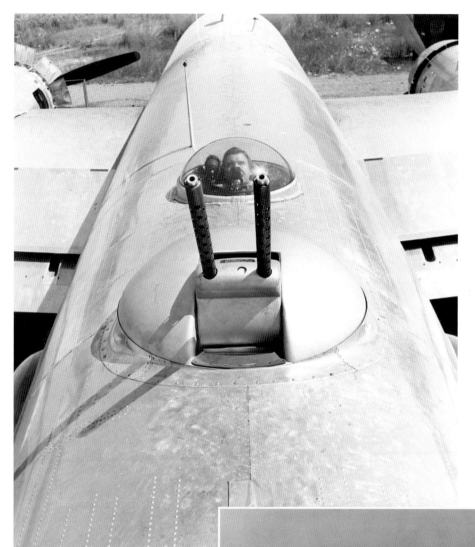

A factory rep operates the top aft turret from the gun-aiming blister. Each .50-caliber (12.7mm) machine gun was equipped with 500 rounds per gun.

The three-gun arrangement (one 20mm and two .50-caliber machine guns) in the tail provided a staggering amount of firepower. Unfortunately, the bullet trajectories between the 20mm cannon and .50-caliber machine guns didn't match, and there was no chance of hitting an enemy fighter with both projectiles at the same time. The 20mm was soon deleted from production B-29s.

B-29s from the 29th Bomb Group head out for another daylight mission against Japan in early 1945. The 29th BG flew its first mission on February 25, 1945, and completed sixty-six combat missions, the last of which was on August 15, 1945.

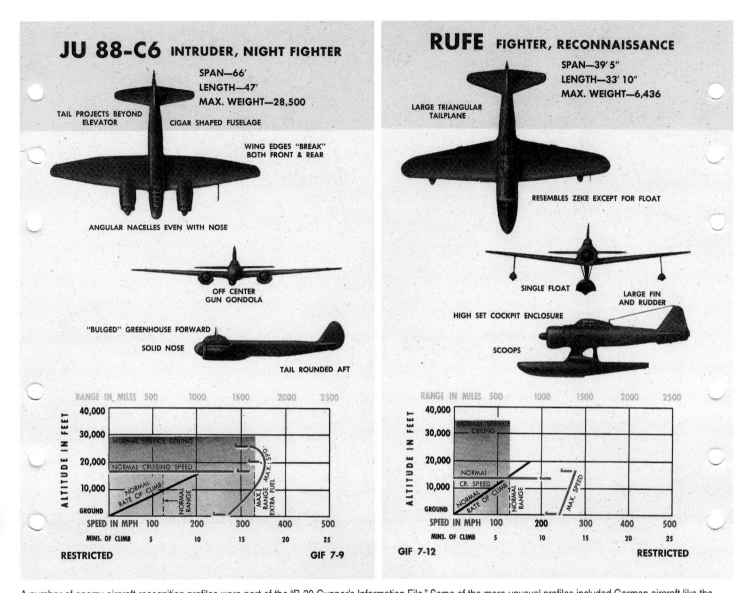

JU 88-C6 INTRUDER, NIGHT FIGHTER

SPAN—66'
LENGTH—47'
MAX. WEIGHT—28,500

TAIL PROJECTS BEYOND ELEVATOR

CIGAR SHAPED FUSELAGE

WING EDGES "BREAK" BOTH FRONT & REAR

ANGULAR NACELLES EVEN WITH NOSE

OFF CENTER GUN GONDOLA

"BULGED" GREENHOUSE FORWARD

SOLID NOSE

TAIL ROUNDED AFT

RANGE IN MILES

ALTITUDE IN FEET

NORMAL SERVICE CEILING

NORMAL CRUISING SPEED

NORMAL RATE OF CLIMB

NORMAL RANGE

MAX. RANGE MAX. SPD. EXTRA FUEL

SPEED IN MPH

MINS. OF CLIMB

GIF 7-9

RUFE FIGHTER, RECONNAISSANCE

SPAN—39' 5"
LENGTH—33' 10"
MAX. WEIGHT—6,436

LARGE TRIANGULAR TAILPLANE

RESEMBLES ZEKE EXCEPT FOR FLOAT

SINGLE FLOAT

LARGE FIN AND RUDDER

HIGH SET COCKPIT ENCLOSURE

SCOOPS

RANGE IN MILES

ALTITUDE IN FEET

NORMAL SERVICE CEILING

NORMAL CR. SPEED

NORMAL RATE OF CLIMB

NORMAL RANGE

MAX. SPEED

SPEED IN MPH

MINS. OF CLIMB

GIF 7-12

A number of enemy aircraft recognition profiles were part of the "B-29 Gunner's Information File." Some of the more unusual profiles included German aircraft like the Ju 88C night fighter and the "Rufe" floatplane fighter—two aircraft the B-29 would never encounter in combat. The B-29 was never intended for combat in Europe, but General Electric, the publishers of the manual, of course would not have been told. As a result, the manual contains recognition profiles for all of the major Luftwaffe and Japanese fighter aircraft.

By January 1945 the RAF had four Meteor IIIs from No. 616 Squadron based at Melsbroek Airfield, Brussels. Frustratingly for the unit, airborne opponents proved elusive, leaving the Meteor pilots to content themselves with strafing ground targets. On March 16, 1945, the RAF had twenty-two Meteor Mk IIIs on strength. Meteor EE275/YQ-Q, seen here, has its engine run up and is parked at airfield B.91, a few miles south of Nijmegen, the Netherlands. TONY BUTLER COLLECTION

This cutaway drawing was produced by Peter Castle and distributed by British Air Intelligence in September 1944. By that time, British ground troops had captured all of the V-1 launch sites in France, ending the first phase of the bombardment. Unfortunately, the aerial assault would continue on London and Antwerp with both air-launched and long-range ground-launched versions of the V-1 until March 29, 1945.

The Bristol Centaurus was one of the best "aero-engines" produced by the British during the Second World War. When first tested in 1938, it was never considered for use in a single-seat fighter and languished behind the famous Merlin. Sydney Camm did fit one into his Tornado prototype and achieved a speed of 421 mph, making it the fastest military aircraft in the world in 1941. The Centaurus would power the Hawker Tempest II and Sea Fury in 1945, but both types were too late to see action in World War II in Europe.

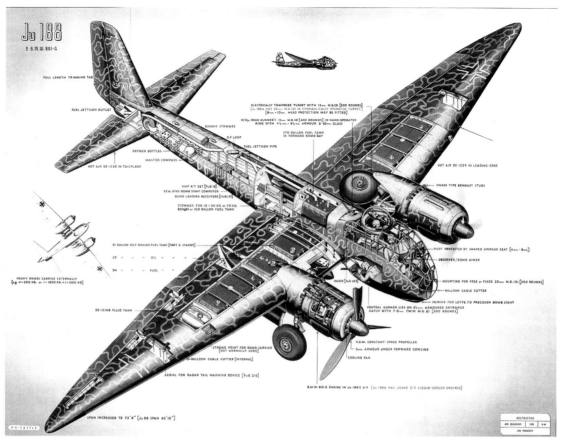

The Ju 188 was arguably the best—and last—medium bomber produced by Germany during the war. On May 10, 1945, just thirty-one Ju 188As were listed as on strength with *III/KG 26* in Norway. How many were serviceable is unknown. The Ju 188 was a great improvement of the famous Ju 88. While 15,000 Ju 88s were produced, only 1,076 Ju 188s left the production line. Impressed by their performance, the New French Air Force put at least thirty Ju 188s back into service in 1945.

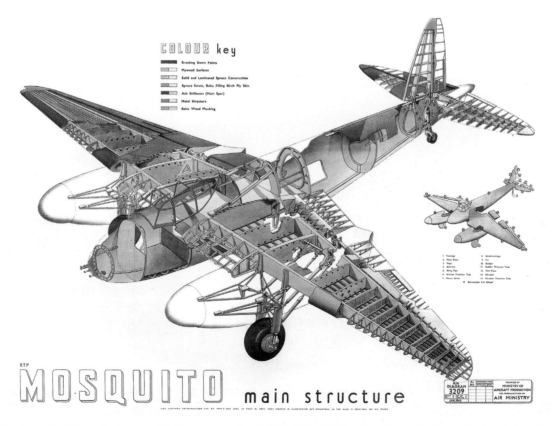

The de Havilland Mosquito was one of the best combat aircraft of World War II. Truly a "wooden wonder," it was the first modern all-wood plane to enter RAF service. The Mosquito was produced quickly and cheaply with nonstrategic materials and was built using a ply-balsa-ply "eggshell" construction. Because of the Mosquito's speed and high ceiling, RAF Bomber Command lost just 260 of the aircraft over 39,795 sorties, for a miniscule loss rate of .65 per sortie—the best of any bomber in the Second World War.

GRIFFON AERO-ENGINE

Two-speed, two-stage supercharger type fitted with Stromberg carburettor

The Rolls Griffon engine was basically a scaled-up Merlin with a capacity of 2,239 cubic inches (36.69 liters) instead of the Merlin's 1,649 cubic inches (26.99 liters). Developing over 2,000 hp, the Griffon would power the Spitfire Mk XIV (entering service in 1944) and the Mk XXI (entering service in April 1945). Luftwaffe general Adolf Galland said after the war, "The best thing about the Spitfire Mk XIV was that there were so few of them."

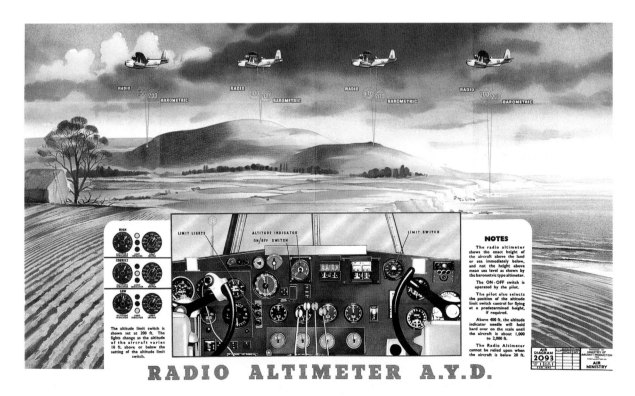

RADIO ALTIMETER A.Y.D.

Radio altimeters were far more accurate than the standard barometric type. The radio altimeter was actually a radar; its downward rays and upward reflections gave exact clearance above the ground or water below.

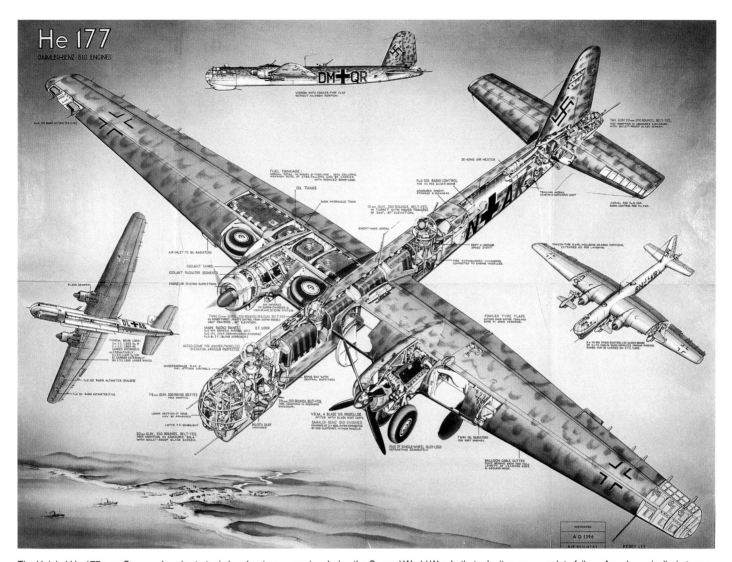

The Heinkel He 177 was Germany's only strategic bomber to see service during the Second World War. In that role, it was a complete failure. Aerodynamically, in terms of handling and performance, the early He 177 was a sound design. Its twin-engine appearance, however, concealed a major flaw: The He 177 was in fact a four-engine bomber, with two coupled engines in each nacelle driving a single propeller. This arrangement was a complete failure, as the engines overheated and frequently caught fire. By January 1945 just a handful of He 177s were still in service with *KG 200* and were used in the antishipping role, armed with the Hs 293 missile.

A No. 421 Squadron RCAF Spitfire Mk XVIE undergoing maintenance in the spring of 1945. Formed in April 1942, No. 421 Squadron was first equipped with the Spitfire Mk VBs. In May the Mk IX replaced the VBs, and in December 1944 the unit was finally equipped with the Mk XVIE clipped-wing version. By the end of the war, the squadron was credited with 92.5 victories.

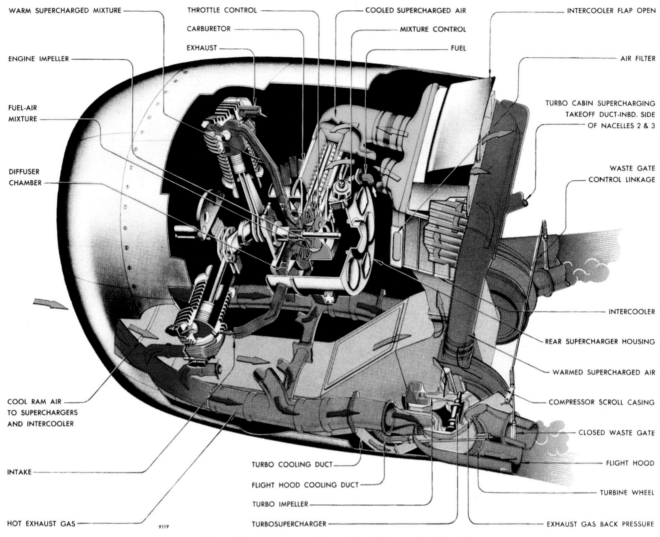

WARM SUPERCHARGED MIXTURE

THROTTLE CONTROL

COOLED SUPERCHARGED AIR

INTERCOOLER FLAP OPEN

CARBURETOR

MIXTURE CONTROL

EXHAUST

FUEL

ENGINE IMPELLER

AIR FILTER

FUEL-AIR
MIXTURE

TURBO CABIN SUPERCHARGING
TAKEOFF DUCT-INBD. SIDE
OF NACELLES 2 & 3

WASTE GATE
CONTROL LINKAGE

DIFFUSER
CHAMBER

INTERCOOLER

REAR SUPERCHARGER HOUSING

WARMED SUPERCHARGED AIR

COOL RAM AIR
TO SUPERCHARGERS
AND INTERCOOLER

COMPRESSOR SCROLL CASING

CLOSED WASTE GATE

FLIGHT HOOD

INTAKE

TURBO COOLING DUCT

FLIGHT HOOD COOLING DUCT

TURBINE WHEEL

TURBO IMPELLER

HOT EXHAUST GAS

9119

TURBOSUPERCHARGER

EXHAUST GAS BACK PRESSURE

Figure 267—Turbosupercharger Flow Diagram (Full Boost)

Taken from the Boeing B-29 pilot's flight manual, this cutaway drawing graphically illustrates the flow of air and gases in the B-29's turbo-supercharger. Each engine had two turbo-superchargers, which boosted the manifold pressure for takeoff and provided increased air pressure at high altitudes.

Newly arrived Spitfire Mk XVIEs of No. 421 and No. 416 Squadrons RCAF dispersed on their snow-covered base at B.56 (Evere) in Belgium in January 1945. The Mk XVI was the same as the Mk IX in nearly all respects except for its engine, a Merlin 266; this was the Merlin 66 built under license in the United States by Packard. Its armament consisted of two 20mm cannon and two .50-caliber machine guns.

HMS Fledgling, in Staffordshire, was home to one of the Women's Royal Naval Service aircraft maintenance training courses in late spring 1945. This photograph shows a Seafire, a Corsair, two Wildcats, two Sea Hurricanes, and a Fairey Fulmar—just a few of the many types of fighter planes the Royal Navy used during World War II.

The business end of a Hispano Mk III 20mm cannon, arguably the best air-to-air weapon built by the Allies during World War II. It was shorter and lighter than the Mk II cannon, with a higher rate of fire.

Two Hispano Mk III 20mm cannon are installed and checked by No. 616 Squadron armorers. Both the Mk I Meteor and Mk III version, which saw service in 1945, were equipped with these weapons. Weighing in at 84 pounds, the Hispano Mk III could fire 350 rounds per minute.

Armorers service a Hispano Mk III 20mm cannon and prepare the ammunition prior to installation. The ammunition load was a fifty-fifty mix of high-explosive and semi-armor-piercing incendiary rounds.

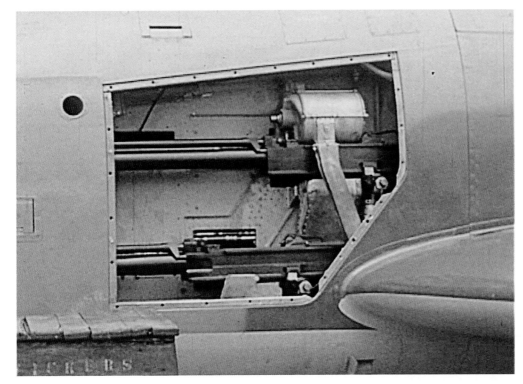

The Meteor Mk III was armed with four Hispano Mk III 20mm cannon with a magazine capacity of 195 rounds per gun, giving the pilot sixteen seconds of firing time.

Rendered obsolete early in the war, the Fairey Battle found a new role as a target tug and trainer for aerial gunners. This Battle, painted in the distinctive high-visibility black-and-yellow color scheme of a target tug, warms up on a snowy ramp in Ontario, Canada, in January 1945. Battles flew thousands of hours as part of the British Commonwealth Air Training Plan.

Engine start-up. This garishly painted 491st Bomb Group B-24 formation assembly ship readies for another mission in late 1945. Equipped with signal lighting and a quantity of flares, each aircraft was painted with a group-specific high-contrast paint scheme of either stripes or polka dots.

A rotte of *III/EJG 2* Me 262a-1as taxi out for a training sortie in early November 1944. *III/EJG 2* was the official training establishment for all future Me 262 fighter pilots; despite fuel shortages and prowling Allied fighters, it operated until being overrun by American troops in April 1945.

This posed shot shows pilots and ground crew in front of a Fleet Air Arm (FAA) Grumman Avenger Mk II (TBM-1/TBM-1C) on the island of Ceylon in 1945. A total of seventeen front-line FAA squadrons flew Avengers during the war, with twenty others providing training or logistics support. Two Royal New Zealand Air Force squadrons also flew the Avenger in the Southwest Pacific until the end of the war. VIA ANDREW THOMAS

This A6M5 Zero from the Technical Air Intelligence Command (TAIC), seen here in early 1945, was used to familiarize newly trained P-38 pilots with their most likely adversary. This Zero was based at AAB Ontario, California, which was well away from metropolitan Los Angeles and offered plenty of airspace for aggressive mock combat.

Well-worn Seafire Mk IIIs line up on deck aboard the HMS *Indefatigable* just weeks after the final surrender in the Pacific. With the war over, the British Pacific Fleet was quickly reduced in strength. These Seafires belong to No. 24 Naval Fighter Wing.

Abandoned IJNAF fighter aircraft litter Atsugi Airfield in September 1945. Closest to the camera is an A6M5c Model 52c Zero. Its tail coding identifies it as belonging to the 302nd Kokutai. On August 15, 1945, the Zeros and J2M3 Raidens of the 302nd were involved in the last dogfights of World War II.

Taken from the tail gunner's position, this color photo show the B-17s of the 385th Bomb Group plowing through heavy flak in January 1945. Smoke markers can be seen above the center B-17; their use indicates this was a "blind bombing" mission using H2S radar.

Ground crew work on Spitfire Mk XI, PM151, of No. 400 Squadron RCAF at B.90 (Petit-Brogel) in Belgium in April 1945. This aircraft is painted in the standard PRU Blue with National Marking III insignia in all positions. The PR Mk XI was capable of 417 mph (671 kph) at 24,000 feet (7,3000 meters).

Based in the Marianas, B-29 *Silver Lady* of the 505th Bomb Group stands ready to receive its load of 1,000-pound general-purpose bombs. Entering combat in February 1945, the 505th bombed targets on Iwo Jima and the Truk Islands. It ended the war dropping supplies to POW camps after VJ-Day.

B-29 air gunners training in a General Electric fire-control simulator. The B-29 was equipped with the world's most advanced computer-aided remote-control turret-gun system. Between June 1944 and August 1945, B-29 gunners were credited with 871 Japanese aircraft shot down, against a loss of 402 B-29s.

B-29s from the 9th Bomb Group climb from their base at Tinian in the North Mariana Islands in the spring of 1945. The B-29 in the foreground is equipped with the AN/APQ-13 ground-scanning radar. Located in the radome between the two bomb bays, the radar was used for high-altitude area bombing and search and navigation.

Gunnery practice in San Diego, California. Gunners fire at towed targets with .50-caliber machine guns on free mounts and truck-mounted turrets. American gunnery schools produced nearly 215,000 gunners, while the British Commonwealth Air Training Program contributed another 34,196.

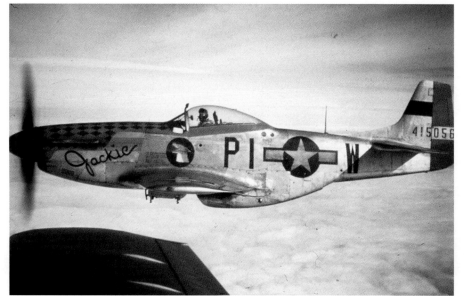

Minus its drop tanks, this 356th Fighter Group P-51D has just completed another long-range escort mission in April 1945. The group consisted of the 359th, 360th, and 361st Fighter Squadrons. The 356th flew its last mission on May 7, 1945, escorting a group of B-17s dropping propaganda leaflets.

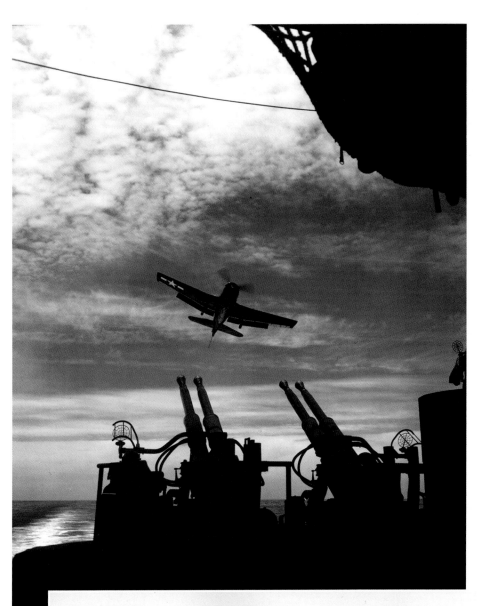

A Grumman F6F-5 Hellcat about to land on the carrier USS *Randolph* in early 1945. The Hellcats of VF-16 were credited with 154.5 enemy aircraft shot down while serving on both the *Lexington* and *Randolph*. VBF-12 was credited with 109 enemy aircraft from January to August 1945 while serving on the *Randolph*.

Canadian Lancaster *S for Smitty* of No. 434 Squadron taxis out in late 1945. Originally equipped with Halifax Vs and Mk IIIs, the unit converted to Lancaster Mk Xs in December 1944. During its tour with No. 6 Group, 434 Squadron flew 2,597 operational sorties on 199 operations and dropped or laid 10,575 tons of bombs and mines, with a loss of 74 aircraft and 68 crews to all causes.

One of the very rare color photographs of a British Supermarine Seafire Mk III in the Pacific. Seen at Clark Field in 1945 in the Philippines, this unidentified Seafire is either a replacement aircraft or was loaned to the Technical Air Intelligence Unit, Southwest Pacific Area, located at Clark Field.

The Japanese air base at Kimpo, Korea, after the Japanese surrender in 1945. The majority of the aircraft in this photo are Tachikawa Ki-55 advanced trainers. By March 1945 all pilot training in both the JAAF and IJNAF had been terminated. GEORGE J. FLEURY VIA WW2COLOR.COM

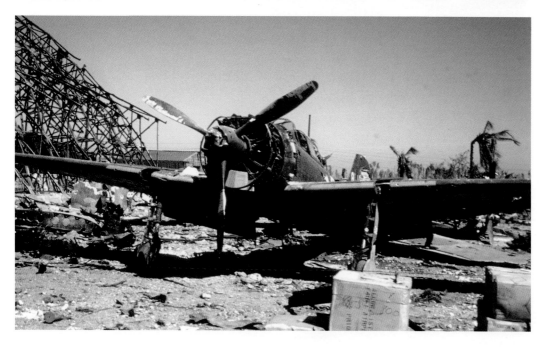

Wherever American and British carrier task forces went, Zero-sens were destroyed in great numbers. The greatest Zero killer was the Grumman F6F Hellcat, with a claimed 13:1 kill ratio against the fabled A6M Zero. This wrecked A6M5 Zero on Kwajalein Atoll in 1945 stands testament to the overwhelming Allied sea power in the Pacific.

THEORY AND PRACTICE—III

"TOJO" — Noticeable features of "Tojo" are the large short nose, the very prominent fairing at the leading-edge root of the wing, the apparent curve on the trailing-edge because of a break in taper, and its short span. The tail projects considerably beyond the tailplane and there is a long and prominent cockpit canopy.

Although individual features are important, don't forget that proportions are equally so. The general proportions of fuselage to wing span and tail should rule out any possible confusion with the Thunderbolt.

This page from the April 1945 issue of *Aircraft Recognition: The Inter-Services Journal* is dedicated to recognizing the noticeable features of the "Tojo"— the Nakajima Ki-44 Shoki single-seat fighter. The Ki-44 would see service with the JAAF on every front except New Guinea and ended the war as an interceptor against the high-flying B-29s.

From the pilot's perspective. B-29s from the 39th Bomb Group, 314th Bomb Wing, release their incendiaries over Hiratsuka on June 16, 1945. The 132 B-29s from the 314th dropped 1,163 tons of incendiaries with no loss of aircraft, although eleven were forced to make emergency landings on Iwo Jima.

By January 1945 the P-38Ls of the 475th Fighter Group were based on Leyte Island in the Philippines. This aircraft belonged to Maj. Oliver S. McAfee, 475th Fighter Group Headquarters, and is seen here on Middelburg Airfield in late 1944.

Capt. Robert Cline flew P-38L-1 135 of the 475th Fighter Group throughout the Philippine Campaign. After twenty-two months of combat operations, the 475th ended the war with 552 aerial victories at the cost of eighty P-38s lost in combat and seventy-five pilots killed in action.

A P-51D of the 318th Fighter Group leads a formation of the USAAF's principal fighters in the Pacific over Saipan in 1945. Second in line is a P-38L, and then a P-47D "razorback." The P-38 was the first to arrive in the Pacific, followed by the P-47 and P-51.

Providing high cover. Lightings of the 49th Fighter Group escort Japanese surrender envoys as they approach le Shima on their way to Manila in the Philippines. The white-painted "Bettys" are accompanied by a B-25 Mitchell from the 499th Bomb Squadron and a B-17H air-sea rescue aircraft carrying an airborne lifeboat.

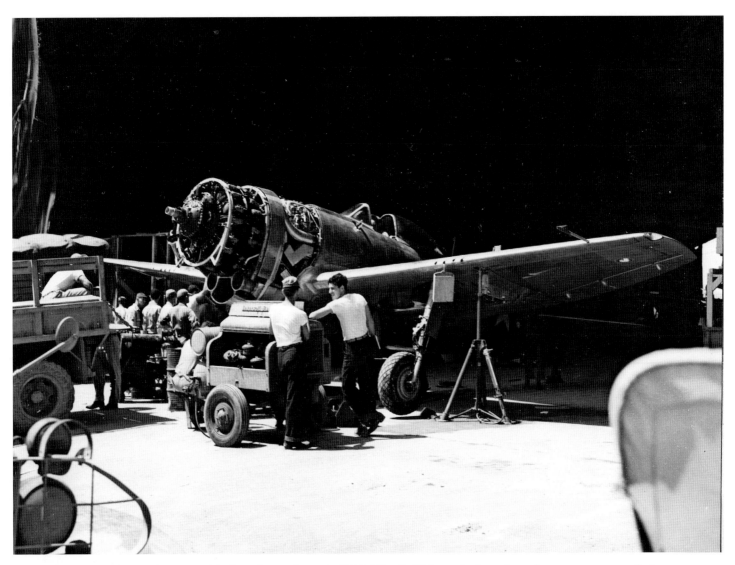

Republic P-47Ns being assembled on Guam in early 1945. The P-47N was designed as a long-range escort fighter for the B-29 in the Pacific, with a more powerful engine, a new turbo-supercharger, more fuel, an automatic pilot, a homing radio, and tail warning radar. The P-47N had a range greater than 1,400 miles—better than the fabled P-51D.

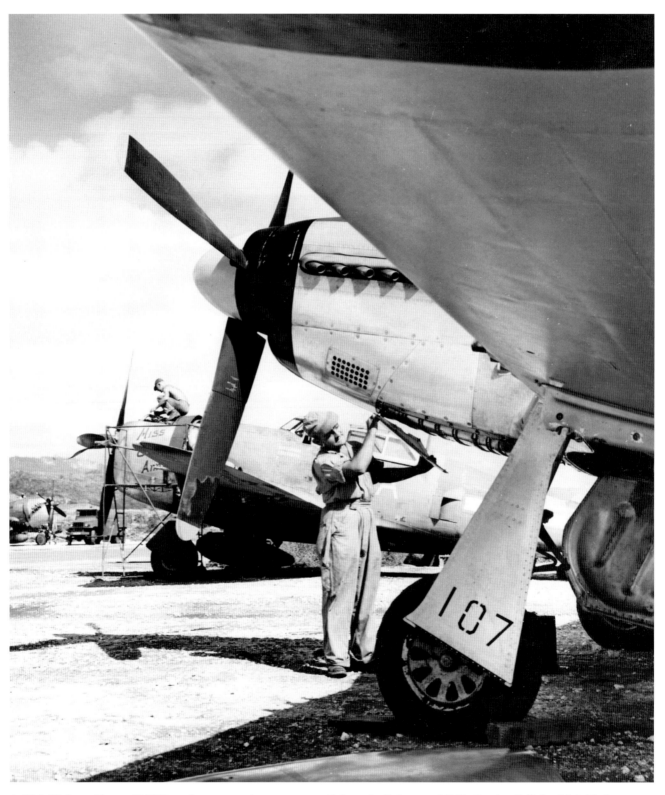

A 15th Fighter Group P-51D undergoes maintenance on Saipan in February 1945. On April 7 the 15th Fighter Group flew its first very long-range (VLR) escort mission to Japan for a force of B-29s assigned to attack the Nakajima aircraft plant near Tokyo.

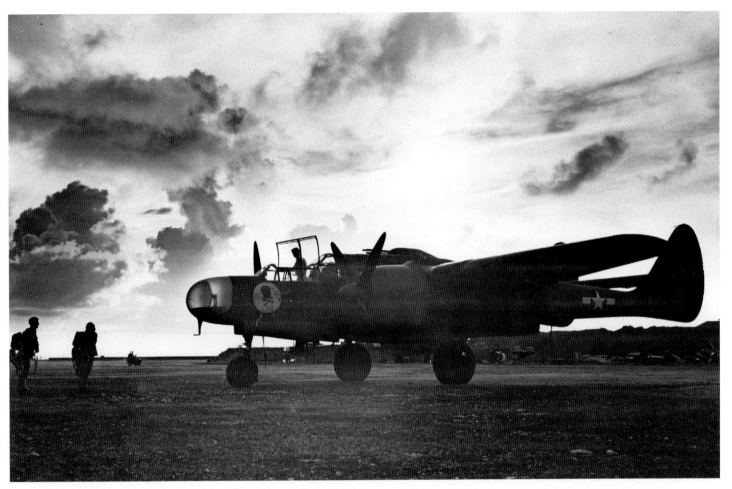

The crew of this P-61A-1 of the 6th Night Fighter Squadron prepare for another nocturnal mission. By 1945 night engagements with Japanese aircraft were sporadic. During the last months of the war, several P-61 squadrons claimed no kills at all. The P-61, however, would lay claim to the last JAAF fighters shot down by a USAAF fighter during the war: on August 14 and 15, a P-61 from the 548th NS shot down a Ki-43 and a Ki-44, respectively.

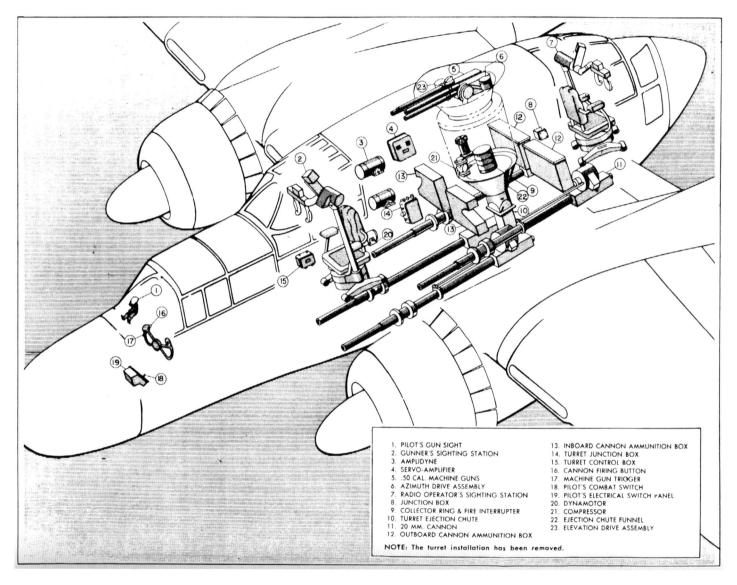

1. PILOT'S GUN SIGHT
2. GUNNER'S SIGHTING STATION
3. AMPLIDYNE
4. SERVO-AMPLIFIER
5. .50 CAL. MACHINE GUNS
6. AZIMUTH DRIVE ASSEMBLY
7. RADIO OPERATOR'S SIGHTING STATION
8. JUNCTION BOX
9. COLLECTOR RING & FIRE INTERRUPTER
10. TURRET EJECTION CHUTE
11. 20 MM. CANNON
12. OUTBOARD CANNON AMMUNITION BOX
13. INBOARD CANNON AMMUNITION BOX
14. TURRET JUNCTION BOX
15. TURRET CONTROL BOX
16. CANNON FIRING BUTTON
17. MACHINE GUN TRIGGER
18. PILOT'S COMBAT SWITCH
19. PILOT'S ELECTRICAL SWITCH PANEL
20. DYNAMOTOR
21. COMPRESSOR
22. EJECTION CHUTE FUNNEL
23. ELEVATION DRIVE ASSEMBLY

NOTE: The turret installation has been removed.

The Northrop P-61 Black Widow was the first and only USAAF night fighter designed for this role during the Second World War. This cutaway drawing shows the P-61's heavy armament of four .50-caliber machine guns housed in a General Electric dorsal barbette and four M2 20mm cannon located in the belly. The P-61 entered service in mid-1944 and saw limited action in Europe and the Pacific. By VJ-Day, 706 had been produced.

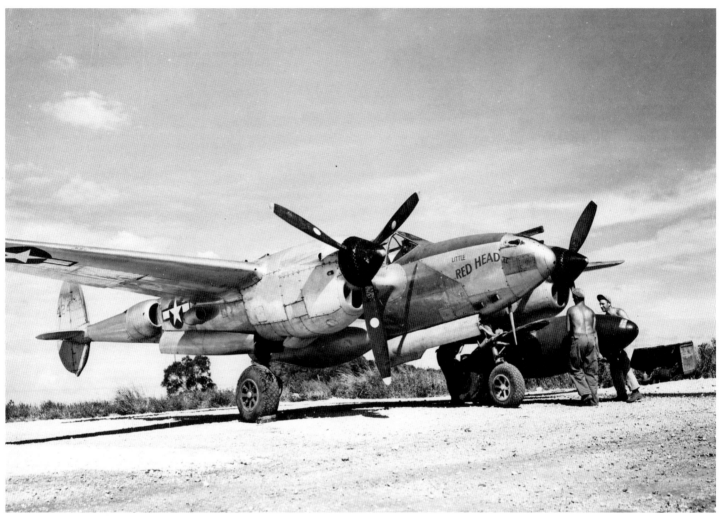

A P-38L is readied for another long-range mission on Saipan in the Marianas. This aircraft is equipped with a single 165-gallon drop tank and a larger 310-gallon tank. This gave the P-38L a fuel capacity of 885 gallons, including the internal fuel load.

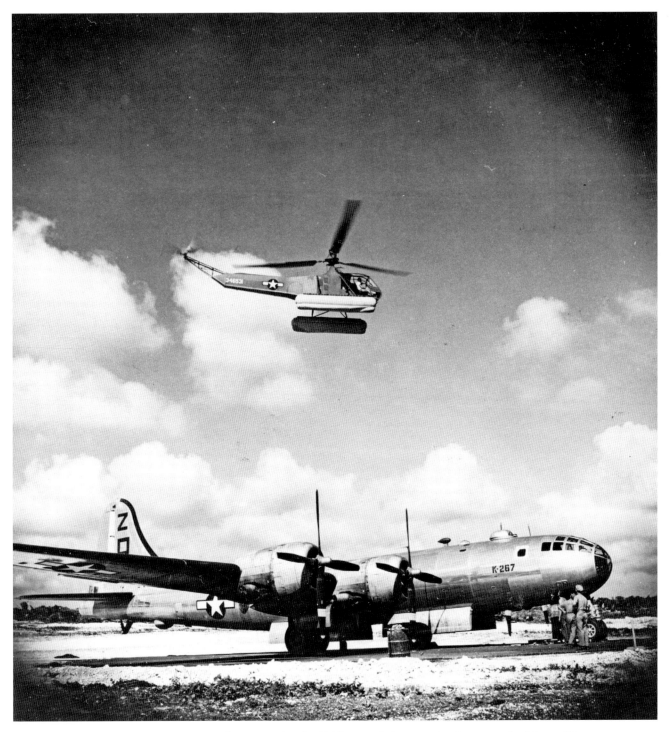

This Sikorsky R-4B helicopter was used as a courier for B-29 parts being serviced on repair ships offshore on Tinian. The R-4B was powered by a single 200 hp Warner R-550-3 engine and equipped with a 38-foot-diameter rotor.

Miss Virgina E from the 9th Photo Reconnaissance Squadron begins another mission from its base at Malir, India, in May 1945. The Lockheed F-5 was the photo-recce version of the famous P-38. Equipped with four K-17 cameras, a drift sight, and autopilot, it proved an excellent reconnaissance aircraft.

120

In the spring of 1945, P-51 Mustang squadrons were moved to Iwo Jima. From there, they provided very long-range escorts for the B-29. By March, however, Maj. Gen. Curtis E. LeMay switched tactics and began a night-bombing campaign against Japanese cities, leaving the P-51s to fly long, boring fighter sweeps over Japan. Here, a B-29 provides navigation and leads a group of P-51s toward Japan.

A Douglas A-20 of the 389th Bomb Squadron, 312th Bomb Group. In the Pacific, the A-20s, like the B-25 Mitchell, were modified into specialized antiship and ground strafers. This 389th BS A-20 has six .50-caliber machine guns mounted in the nose. By 1945 Japanese fighter resistance was almost nonexistent, and their flak defenses never reached the level encountered by Allied pilots flying over Europe and Germany. MIKE BUTRY

Three B-25Hs of the Tenth Air Force ready for takeoff from their base at Hailakandi, India. The B-25H was extremely heavily armed, with one T13E1 75mm and eight forward-firing .50-caliber machine guns.

Immediately after the former Japanese air bases in and around Hollandia, New Guinea, were captured, they were developed into a major U.S. Army base and staging area in preparation for the invasion of the Philippines. Here, Douglas A-20s of the 312th Bomb Group are seen just prior to leaving Hollandia and joining the fight in the Philippines in 1945. MIKE BUTRY

The last North American B-25H produced during the war was given the name *Bones* and signed by hundreds of company employees. It was issued to the 81st Bomb Group stationed in India in 1945.

A P-47D of the 1st Air Commando loaded with three 1,000-pound bombs. This was one of the heaviest loads carried by the P-47 and equal to that carried by Japanese medium bombers at the beginning of the war.

A Tenth Air Force P-51A loaded with two 1,000-pound bombs and two M-10 triple 4.5-inch rocket tubes. The 4.5-inch rockets were popular with Tenth Air Force units, which often had to attack small, well-hidden jungle targets, as they proved more accurate than freefall bombs.

Irish Lassie of the 459th "Twin Dragon" Fighter Squadron is loaded with an unusual piece of ordnance: an AN-MK47 350-pound depth charge. On February 11, 1945, the 459th scored its last aerial victory of the war by shooting down a Ki-61 "Tony."

Modified from the B-17G, the B-17H search-and-rescue variant was equipped with airborne search radar and an air-droppable rescue boat. This B-17H belongs to the 6th Emergency Rescue Squadron based at Floridablanca Airfield in Luzon, the Philippines, in June 1945.

Consolidated B-32 Dominators of the 312th Bomb Group, 386th Bomb Squadron, at Luzon, the Philippines, in June 1945. Three test B-32s were assigned to the 312th and on May 29 the first combat mission was flown. The 312th BG flew just thirteen combat missions before the end of the war.

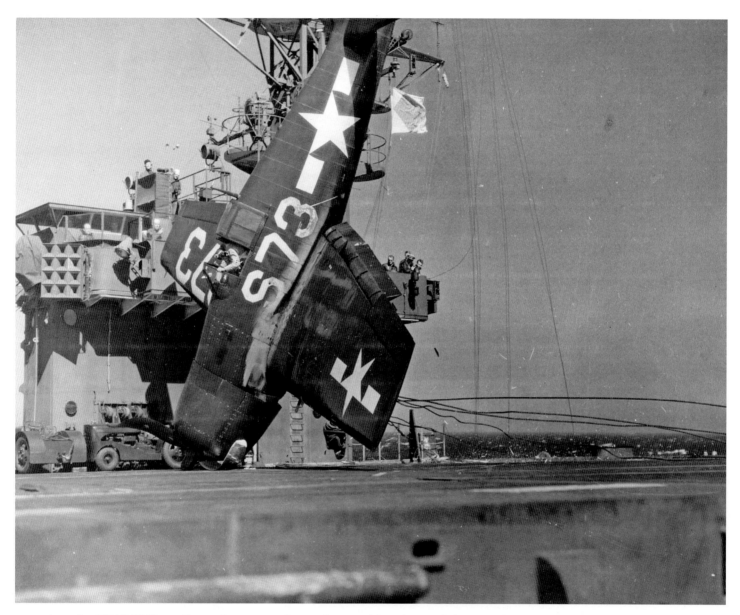

A novice F6F-5 Hellcat pilot ends up nose-down after catching the crash barrier aboard the USS *Takanis*. Operating out of San Diego, the *Takanis* was used exclusively for training; between May 1944 and August 1945, she qualified 2,509 navy aviators.

The night-torpedo version of the Grumman Avenger was designated TBM-3D. Equipped with the RT-5/APS-4 search radar, operating at 3cm wavelength in a pod outboard on the right wing, the TBM-3D was the best-equipped Avenger of the war. Here, seven TBM-3Ds of Night Torpedo Squadron VT(N)-90 from the carrier USS *Enterprise* fly in formation. BARRETT TILLMAN

TBM Avengers from USS *Suwannee* drop 500-pound bombs on Shigaki Airfield in April 1945. During the battle for Okinawa, the Avengers from *Suwannee* had the unenviable task of preventing the Japanese from using their airbases on the Sakishima Islands. Airfields were hard to destroy, leading to repeated attacks. In all, the Avengers spent seventy-seven days attacking these airfields.

An F8F Bearcat aboard the USS *Charger* undergoes carrier trials in February 1945. Too late to see action, the F8F was a remarkable fighter and the last in a long line of piston-engine fighters produced by Grumman.

F4U-1D Corsairs aboard USS *Essex* prepare for another airfield strike on the island of Formosa in January 1945. The *Essex* was equipped with two U.S. Marine Corsair squadrons. Early offensive fighter sweeps were conducted without ordnance; rockets and bombs were used later.

Landing aboard the USS *Franklin*, an F4U-1D's drop tank breaks free and explodes in a huge ball of flame. Both the pilot and plane survived.

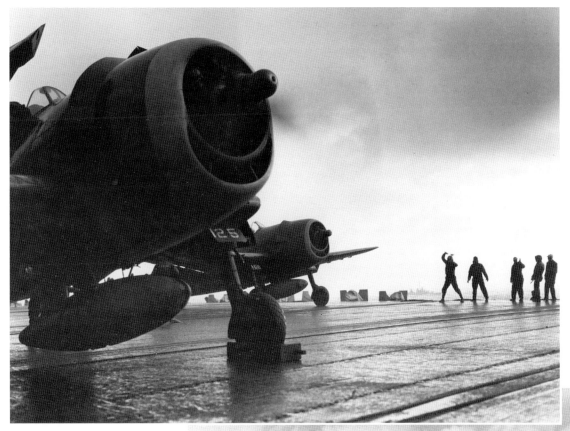

On February 16, 1945, F6F-5 Hellcats aboard the USS *Essex* warm up for the first carrier strike against Tokyo. Fleet Admiral Chester Nimitz's communiqué announcing the strike stated: "This operation has long been planned and the opportunity to accomplish it fulfills the deeply cherished desire of every officer and man in the Pacific Fleet."

The Consolidated PB4Y-2 Privateer patrol bomber was developed from the B-24 and featured a lengthened and completely redesigned rear fuselage. Its armament consisted of twelve .50-caliber machine guns in four turrets and two waist blisters.

This dramatic shot shows a section of four F6F-5s from USS *Yorktown* making a low-level run over Iwo Jima on February 21, 1945. The Hellcats from the *Yorktown* would support the Iwo Jima landings until February 23 before returning to air strikes against Japan proper.

The end of the *Yamato*. In the last major air attack of the war on Japanese naval vessels, the Japanese Imperial Navy sent the super battleship *Yamato*, the light cruiser *Yahagi*, and a squadron of destroyers on a one-way mission. On April 7, 1945, this force was attacked by 386 aircraft from Task Force 38. In this photo, a Helldiver circles the smoking *Yamato*. In the end, the *Yamato*, the *Yahagi*, and four destroyers were lost that day, as well as seven Helldivers.

By July 1945 both the JAAF and JNAF had all but ceded air superiority to the Allies. With the Imperial Navy no longer a threat, U.S. and Royal Navy carrier groups were free to concentrate air strikes against airfields and coastal targets. These smoking "Bettys" at Honshu Airfield attest to the Allies' overpowering presence.

The Japanese battleship *Haruna* under attack on July 28. At the beginning of 1945, the *Haruna* was left immobile at Kure in Japanese waters. After being damaged by U.S. carrier strikes in March, she was finally sunk by Task Force 38 aircraft in the July attack.

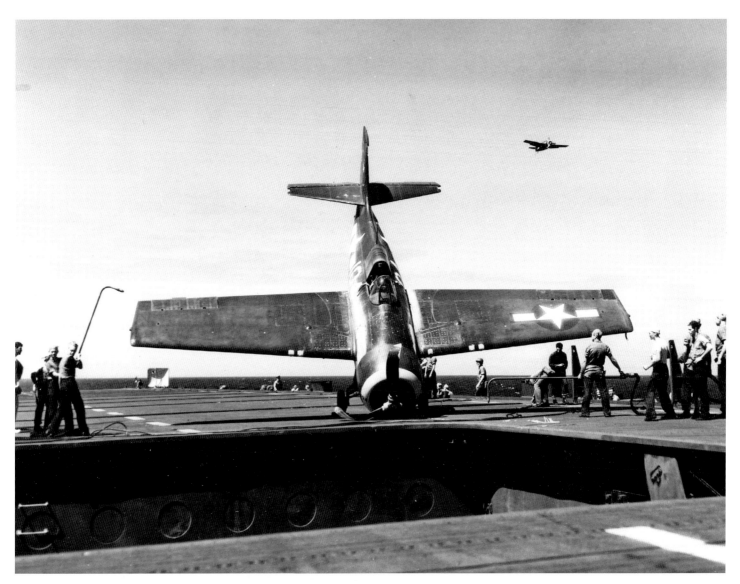

Deck crew stand ready in case of fire when an FM-2 Wildcat goes nose-up after landing aboard the USS *Shipley Bay* in February 1945. The FM-2 was the ultimate version of the Wildcat to see service during the war. Earmarked for the growing escort carrier force, the FM-2 proved a tough and reliable fighter. By VJ-Day, the total Wildcat score stood at 1,514.5 aerial victories.

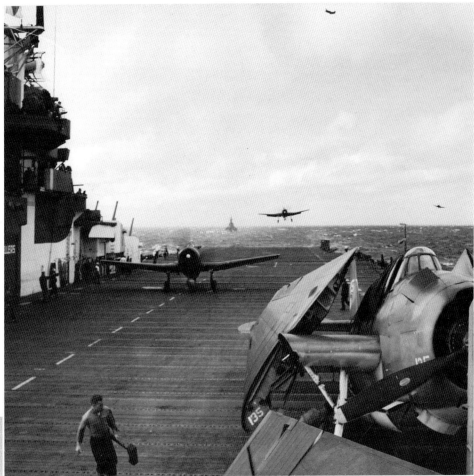

F6F-5 Hellcats from the USS *Hornet* return after a predawn strike on Tokyo in February 1945. This photo clearly illustrates the high tempo required for carrier operations. The first Hellcat has just landed and moves forward; another is about to land, with a third curving into its final approach.

On May 11, 1945, the carrier USS *Bunker Hill* was hit by two bombs along with the two kamikaze aircraft that dropped them. Prior to the attack, the flight deck was crowded with thirty-four aircraft ready for another strike. The damage was so extensive that the *Bunker Hill* had to retire for repairs. She was still under repair when the war ended.

A Martin PBM-5 Mariner on the ramp at Sangley Point in the Philippines. In the foreground is the wrecked fuselage of a Mitsubishi F1M "Pete." The PBM-5 was a relatively unknown type compared to the Consolidated PBY Catalina and was built in smaller numbers. Its performance, however, was superior, and it was used as a patrol bomber and rescue aircraft. It also had the honor of participating in all the major offensive campaigns in the Pacific.

A pair of SB2C Helldivers from the carrier USS *Hancock* head to their target over Iwo Jima in February 1945. During the war, the SB2Cs fell well short of original expectations. In the last seven months of 1945, 496 Helldivers were lost to all causes, although that number included eighty "war wearies" scrapped at Pearl Harbor.

TBM Avengers of Torpedo Squadron Four, Task Group 38.3, of the USS *Essex*, on their way to shipping and airfield targets in the Saigon area on January 12, 1945. Torpedo Squadron Four was one of the few U.S. Navy Avenger squadrons to see service in both Europe and the Pacific.

The final surrender papers of World War II were signed aboard the USS *Missouri* (BB-63) on September 2, 1945. Shortly after, the largest aerial formation ever assembled—consisting of 2,000 aircraft—flew over in celebration.

CHAPTER 5

SOVIET UNION

A Soviet Il-2M in flight. The Il-2 Shturmovik was the most numerous ground-attack aircraft produced in World War II. Well armed (two 23mm cannon) and well armored (the cockpit was shielded by plates between 5mm and 12mm thick), the Il-2 unfortunately was like all ground-attack aircraft of World War II—inaccurate, particularly with bombs. To compensate, the Soviets concentrated massive numbers of Shturmoviks in order to support their ground operations.

Russian PE2-1s of the 3rd Bomber Air Corps hit German targets near Bobruisk on
the Belorussian Front in late 1944. The PE-2 was one of the finest twin-engine light
bombers of the war and saw action from the first day of the war to the very last.
GENNADY SLOUTSKI

By January 1945 Soviet V-VS air strength exceeded 15,000 aircraft. During the ensuing winter offensive, the Luftwaffe responded with some 650 fighters and over 100 close-support Fw 190Fs. These had little impact, however, as formations of Il-2s (shown here) and well-flown La-7s, Yak-3s, and Yak-9Ds overwhelmed both German ground and air forces.

A group of Tupolev Tu-2s of the 334rd Bomber Air Division head to their target. The Tu-2 did not enter service until January of 1944 and saw its final action against the Japanese Kwantung Army in August 1945. GENNADY SLOUTSKI

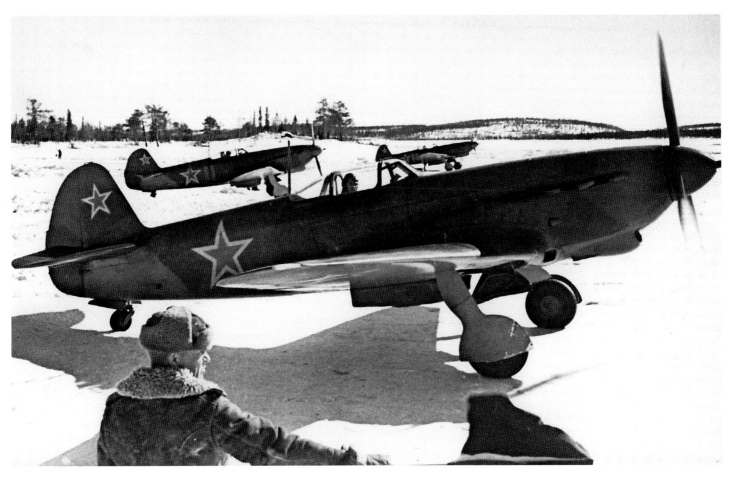

Three Yakovlev Yak-9Ds in the winter of 1945. Produced in larger numbers than any other Russian fighter, the Yak-9 saw continuous action from October 1942 until the end of the war. GENNADY SLOUTSKI

The Lavochkin La-7 was one of the finest Russian fighters of the war. At low level, the La-7 was capable of outrunning both the Bf 109 and Fw 190. In the final weeks of the war, "free hunt" regiments of the VVS-KA equipped with La-7s proved devastating against the remaining low-flying Fw 190s and Bf 109s. GENNADY SLOUTSKI

Roughly equal to the Heinkel He 111 in terms of performance, range, and bomb load, the Ilyushin Il-4 was the first Soviet bomber to raid Berlin and served until the end of the war. Here, an Il-4B is cleared for takeoff in the spring of 1945.

CHAPTER 6
JAPAN

The Ki-100-I-Ko *Goshikisen* of the 1st Chutai of the 59th Sentai was one of the best piston-engine fighters of World War II. Here, a group sits at readiness at Ashiya Airfield in Fukuoka Prefecture, Japan, in June 1945.

Known as the "Tony II," the Ki-100 was a quick improvisation with a Ki-61 airframe married to a Mitsubishi Ha-112-II fourteen-cylinder, air-cooled, radial engine. The Ki 100-I-*Otsu* had an all-around-vision hood. Just eighty-eight were built before aerial attacks ended production.

This Ki-100-I-*Otsu*, *White 39*, was the personal mount of Maj. Yasuhida Baba, Hikotai-cho of the 5th Sentai. During operations in 1945, the 5th Sentai claimed forty B-29s destroyed and more than a hundred damaged—all for a loss of ten pilots killed and six in operational accidents.

A Ki-46-III-Kai of the 16th Independent Chutai at Taisho Airfield in early 1945. The KAI Type 100 fighter was a modification of the Ki-46-III reconnaissance aircraft. Fitted with a new nose, it contained two 20mm Ho-5 cannon and a single 37mm Ho-202 cannon in the center fuselage, firing upward at an angle of 60 degrees. The Ki-46-III-Kai was not a success due to its slow rate of climb.

Kawasaki Ki-61-I-*KAIcs* of the 244th Sentai at Chofti. Tasked with providing protection for the Tokyo area, the 244th Sentai gained considerable fame against the B-29s, claiming over twenty-six by the end of the war.

Two unidentified Ki-61-I-*Teis*, possibly from the 19th Sentai, in the Philippines in 1945. The aircraft in the foreground is equipped with two 53-gallon drop tanks. The *Tei* featured two 12.7mm machine guns in the strengthened wing and wing racks for external stores.

Near the end of the war, many countries formerly occupied by the Japanese scrambled to rebuild their air forces. The Kawasaki Ki-61-*KAIc* "Tony" was one of many ex-Japanese aircraft pressed into service; this one was photographed on November 16, 1945, at Peiping by Chinese Communists.

Kawasaki's attempt to improve on the already excellent DB 601A engine ended in failure. The new Ha-140 engine, seen here on the front end of a Ki 61-II, proved to be one of the most unreliable and troublesome engines of any Japanese fighter. Developing 1,500 hp, the new Ki-61-II's performance was disappointing and only eight of the eleven built were ever test-flown.

Captured Japanese aircraft were thoroughly tested by the Technical Air Intelligence Center (TAIC). This Kawanishi Ki-61-Ia was captured on Cape Gloucester in 1943 and shipped to the United States from Australia. On July 2, 1945, it was forced to belly-land due to engine failure. The Ki-61 "Tony" was the only liquid-cooled powered fighter to enter service with the JAAF and saw action until the end of the war.

Japanese ground crew under Allied supervision stand in front of a captured Mitsubishi J2M3 Raiden in Malaya, 1945. The Mitsubishi J2M3 was designed by Jiro Horikoshi, creator of the A6M Zero. It was intended from the outset as an interceptor with speed, rate of climb, and armament paramount. Unfortunately, the J2M suffered from a series of teething problems related to the Kasei engine, the propeller pitch-change mechanism, and the landing gear. By war's end, only 625 had been built.

Two captured Mitsubishi J2M3s in flight with the ATAIU-SEA 1945. The Allied Technical Air Intelligence Unit—South East Asia was formed at Maiden, India, in 1943 and was a combined RAF/USAAF unit before USAAF personnel were transferred back to the States. By early 1946, sixty-four captured Japanese Army and Navy aircraft, most in flyable condition, were based in Singapore. Lack of shipping prevented all but four aircraft from being shipped back to the United Kingdom.

Two Mitsubishi J2M3 Raidens from the ATAIU-SEA bank for the camera. These two examples, tail codes B1-01 and B1-02, were captured at the end of the war and belonged to the 381st Kokutai.

A mix of captured Mitsubishi J2M3s and A6M5c Model 52cs at Atsugi Airfield near Tokyo. The propellers have been removed to prevent any misuse by Japanese personnel.

These Mitsubishi J2M3s belong to the 1st Hikotai of the 302nd Kokutai at Atsugi Airfield in early 1945. Operating a mixed force of both Zeros and J2M3 "Jacks," the 302nd Kokutai flew in defense of Tokyo, but by May the unit was down to just ten operational aircraft. On August 15 it flew its last combat mission, engaging Hellcats from VF-88 just two hours before the surrender announcement. HENRY SAKAIDA

War prizes. A number of Mitsubishi Zeros aboard the USS *Copahee* bound for the United States in late 1945. The Zero-sen closest to the camera is an A5M5b Type 52b model, identified by the larger gunport on the right side of the cowling. This was enlarged to accommodate the Type 3 13.2mm machine gun.

A Mitsubishi A6M6c Model 53c was fitted with the Sakae Model 31 A engine with water-methanol injection, which proved unreliable, and performance suffered as a result. Only one Model 53c was built.

The inability of the Japanese to produce a replacement for the Zero-sen meant its fighter pilots were forced to fly the A6M to the very end. This A6M5c Model 52c is one of the 1,578 Zero-sens produced between January and July 1945.

A6M5c Type 52cs of the 252nd Kokutai warm up in preparation for another mission in the summer of 1945. Considered obsolete by 1945, the Zero-sen was still a formidable opponent when flown by a skilled and experienced pilot. HENRY SAKAIDA

164 AIR COMBAT 1945

At the time of surrender in August 1945, Japanese troops were instructed to paint over the red Hinomaru ("circle of the sun") and replace it with a green cross on all aircraft. This Zero-sen has a white background and the green cross.

This Zero-sen kamikaze carrying a 550-pound bomb was photographed diving on the USS *Enterprise* in May 1945. During 1945 the USS *Enterprise* was hit twice by kamikaze aircraft. After March 1945, more than half of the Japanese pilots available sacrificed themselves in these attacks.

102D-3

ZEKE 52

FIELDS OF FIRE

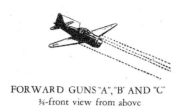

FORWARD GUNS "A", "B" AND "C"
¾-front view from above

EXHAUST FLAME PATTERNS

REAR VIEW

VULNERABILITY

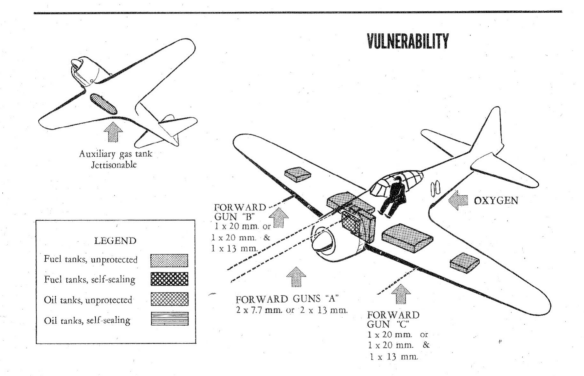

Auxiliary gas tank
Jettisonable

LEGEND

Fuel tanks, unprotected
Fuel tanks, self-sealing
Oil tanks, unprotected
Oil tanks, self-sealing

FORWARD
GUN "B"
1 x 20 mm. or
1 x 20 mm. &
1 x 13 mm.

FORWARD GUNS "A"
2 x 7.7 mm. or 2 x 13 mm.

FORWARD
GUN "C"
1 x 20 mm. or
1 x 20 mm. &
1 x 13 mm.

OXYGEN

ARMAMENT

	No.	Size	Rds. Gun	Type		No.	Size	Rds. Gun	Type
Forward Cowl	2	7.7 mm or	700	Fixed	Tail				
Top	2	13.2 mm		Fixed	Wing	2	20 mm or	100	Fixed
Side						2	20 mm and	100	Fixed
Bottom						2	13.2 mm		Fixed

TACTICAL DATA

DATE March 1945

A Technical Air Intelligence Command 102D Performance and Characteristics report for the Zeke 52. Issued in March 1945, the A6M5 Model 52 had been in production since 1943. It was designed to simplify and speed up production, as well as increase its diving speed. The A6M5 Model 52 was the most widely used, with 1,701 built.

102D-2

PERFORMANCE AND CHARACTERISTICS

ZEKE 52

TAKE-OFF

	Load	Feet
Runway Requirements	6026	975
T.O. over 50' obstacle		
Landing over 50' obstacle		
* T.O. + 100%		

CLIMB—CEILING

@ 6026 lbs.	Feet	Min.
Rate @ S.L.	3140	1
Rate @ 8,000 ft.	3340	1
Time to 10,000'		3.6
Time to 20,000'		7.8
Service ceiling	35,100'	

AIRCRAFT

Duty Fighter

Designation Type 0 Model 52

Description Low-wing Monoplane

Mfg. Mitsubishi & Nakajima

Engines 1   Crew 1

Construction All Metal

SPEED

@ 6026 lbs.	Mph.	Knts.	Altitude
Maximum WE	295	256	@ S.L.
Maximum WE	358	310	@ 22,000'
Military	351	304	23,100'
Cruising			
Economical			

BOMBS—CARGO

	No.	Size	Total Lbs.
Normal			
Maximum	2	60 kg	264
or	10	32 kg	704

ENGINES

	H.P.	Altitude
Take-off	1120	S.L.
Normal	830	1500'
Military	1080	9300'
	950	21600'
War Emerg.	1210	8000'

Mfg. Nakajima

Model Sakae 31 A

Type Radial

Cylinders 14   Cooling Air

Supercharger 2 Speed

Propeller 3-Blade Diam. 10'
C.S.

Fuel - Take-off 92 Cruising 92

WEIGHTS

	Lbs.
Empty	4236
Gross Normal	6026
Overload	6600

FUEL

	U.S. gal.	Imp. gal.
Built-in	156	129
Internal (Removable)		
External (drop)	87	72
Maximum	243	201

DIMENSIONS

Span 36.1'   Length 29.8'
Height 9.2'   Wing area 230 sq.ft.

RANGE AND RADIUS

	Miles		Speed		Alt. feet	Fuel gal.		Bombs lbs.	Cargo lbs.
	stat.	naut.	mph.	Knts.		U.S.	Imp.		
Maximum range (maximum fuel)	1844	1600	146	126	1500	243	201	None	None
At 75% Vmax.	1478	1630	198	172	1500	243	201	None	None
Maximum range (normal fuel)	1200	1042	146	126	1500	156	129	None	None
At 75% Vmax.	948	823	202	175	1500	156	129	None	None
Radius ( )									
Radius ( )									

GENERAL DATA

A maximum speed of only 340 mph has been obtained in flight tests.

DATE March 1945

This rather poor-quality, air-to-air shot shows four A6M2-K Zero-sen trainers. By May–June 1945, the primary concern of the IJNAF and JAAF was the invasion of the Japanese mainland. To that end, nearly 10,700 aircraft and 18,000 pilots were assigned as kamikazes; many would have flown in the A6M2-K.

An early-morning flight for two Kawanishi N1K2-J Shiden *Kais* in 1945. These two captured "Georges" prepare for a ferry flight to Yokosuka. The largest quantity of serviceable NIK2-Js were found at the Omura Naval Base shortly after the surrender.

A captured Yokosuka MXY-7 Model 22 *Ohka* kamikaze antishipping attack plane. Powered by the Ishikawajima Tsu-11 thermojet engine, the Model 22 was loaded with a 1,300-pound warhead and was to be carried by the Yokosuka P1Y1 "Ginga" bomber. Only fifty were built.

The Nakajima Ki-115 was a purpose-built kamikaze aircraft made from wood and steel. By the end of the war, thousands of JAAF and IJNAF planes and pilots were used as kamikazes.

In response to the high-altitude threat posed by the B-29, the JAAF ordered the production of the Nakajima Ki-87 with an exhaust-driven turbo-supercharger. This was the only one ever built. The Ki-87 had an estimated speed of 433 mph at 36,090 feet.

The Nakajima Ki-87 was powered by a Mitsubishi Ha.215 (Ha.44/21) eighteen-cylinder radial engine rated at 2,400 hp for takeoff and 1,850 hp at 34,500 feet.

Nakajima Ki-84-1a *Hayates* of the 2nd Chutai, 73rd Sentai, are seen here in late 1944. Rushed into service in May of 1944, this unit would virtually cease to exist by March 1945.

The state of fighter art. This mixed formation, led by a captured Nakajima Ki-84 *Hayate* "Frank," represents fighter technology in 1945. These examples are flown by the Technical Air Intelligence Unit based at Clark Field in the Philippines in January 1945 and include a P-51D, a F6F-5 Hellcat, and a Seafire Mk III.

A Nakajima Ki-84-1a "Frank" of the 111th Sentai. Organized in July 1945, the 111th Sentai was one of the last JAAF units formed during the war.

The Ki-84-1a was the best JAAF fighter of the war. Shortly after hostilities, a small number served with the Chinese Communists, adorned with the white-and-blue starburst insignia of the Chinese Air Force.

The 84th Airdrome Squadron landed at Hollandia, New Guinea, on May 13, 1944. During that month, the 84th Squadron began the painstaking job of rebuilding two Japanese Nakajima Ki-43-II *Hayabusa* "Oscars." The aircraft were test-flown in August and September and handed over to the Air Technical Intelligence Unit for further study. MIKE BUTRY

One of the 84th Airdrome Squadron's Ki-43-II "Oscars" under maintenance in
Hollandia, 1944–45. The Ki-43 served from the first day of the war to the very last,
but by 1945 it was clearly obsolete. With a top speed of just 320 mph at 19,680 feet
and armed with two 12.7mm machine guns, the Ki-43-II was completely outclassed
by every fighter the Allies had in 1945. MIKE BUTRY

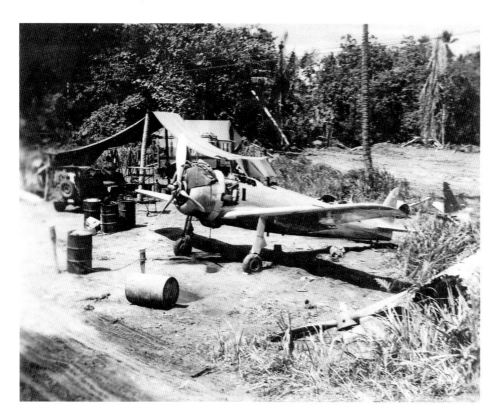

An unidentified Ki-43 "Oscar" of the 84th Airdrome Squadron undergoes
maintenance sometime in 1944–45. All airworthy captured enemy aircraft were
handed over to the local Air Technical Intelligence Unit for further study. Some
were test-flown on-site, while others were earmarked for shipment to the United
States or Australia. MIKE BUTRY

Hollandia 1945. By the end of the war, wrecked Japanese aircraft were ubiquitous on captured airfields. This JAAF Kawasaki Ki-48 light bomber was one of the thousands of Japanese aircraft abandoned or destroyed by Allied airpower. MIKE BUTRY

By 1942 the Kawasaki Ki-48 light bomber was clearly obsolete and would all but disappear from the skies in 1945. These two wrecked Ki-84s were pushed aside by the 84th Airdrome Squadron in 1945. MIKE BUTRY

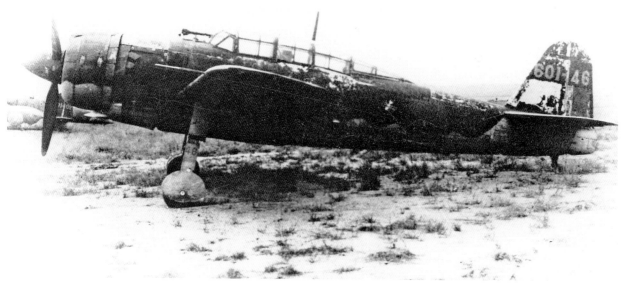

By 1945 the Yokosuka D4Y3 *Suisei* "Judy" was used almost exclusively as a kamikaze. Its most noticeable success occurred on March 18, 1945, when D4Y3s damaged both the USS *Enterprise* and USS *Yorktown*.

The Mitsubishi Ki-67 Type 4 *Hiryu* heavy bomber, code-named "Peggy," entered service in late 1944 with little or no impact. Just 698 were produced, with a small number used as kamikazes in the last few months of the war.

The Tachikawa Ki-74 "Patsy," seen here in the United States shortly after hostilities ended, was one of Japan's most advanced bombers. Designed with exceptional range, it was capable of bombing the United States from Japan's most forward operating bases.

A camouflaged Nakajima Ki-44 *Shoki* of the 246th Sentai found abandoned in the Philippines. In December 1944 the survivors of the 246th Sentai returned to Japan to reequip with the Ki-44. Both the 70th Sentai and the 246th would use them as night fighters against the B-29s in 1945.

Three Ki-44s of the 70th Sentai use a Toyota KC truck for startup. By 1945 the units equipped with the Ki-44 represented 18 percent of the JAAF fighter airpower dedicated to home defense. A total of 1,228 Ki-44s were produced during the war.

Built but never flown—the prototype of the Tachikawa Ki-94-II high-altitude fighter was still under construction when the war ended. Powered by an Ha-219ru (Ha-44-12) air-cooled radial rated at 2,240 hp, it had an estimated speed of 438 mph at 39,370 feet.

This splendid air-to-air shot shows a Kawasaki Ki-45-Kai-Hei of the 3rd Chutai, 53rd Sentai, on patrol. From its airfield at Matsudo near Tokyo, the 3rd Chutai was assigned air defense against the high-flying B-29. This aircraft has a pair of obliquely mounted (at an angle of 70 degrees) Ho-5 20mm cannon fitted in place of the 59-Imperial-gallon upper fuselage tank.

An RAF officer examines an abandoned Ki-45 *Toryu* "Nick" of the 71st Dokuritsu Hiko Chutai. These aircraft were found at Kallang Airfield, Singapore, in September 1945.

The Nakajima B6N2 *Tenzan* "Jill" torpedo bomber. Making their carrier debut during the disastrous Battle of the Philippine Sea, June 19–20, 1944, the B6N2s failed to inflict any damage on the U.S. fleet. By 1945 Japan's carrier force was no longer a threat, leaving the B6N2 to operate from shore bases. During the Battle of Okinawa, the B6N2 was also used for kamikaze missions for the first time.

A Nakajima B6N2 seen here at Atsugi Airfield shortly after the war. This aircraft is equipped with the 3-Shiki Type 3 air-to-surface radar. The antennas were installed along the leading edge of the wings and the sides of the fuselage.

The Kawasaki Ki-97, designed as a more powerful fighter based on the success of the Ki-45 *Toryu*, was the third prototype produced and tested in 1944. By 1945 just a handful of Ki-97s were kept in reserve for the coming invasion of Japan.

A Nakajima G5N2 "Liz" is seen here at Atsugi Airfield shortly after hostilities. Designed as a navy long-range attack bomber, the G5N proved disappointing, with just six completed. Four were converted to navy transports as G5N2s and equipped with Nakajima NK7A Mamori 11 radial engines and four-blade propellers.

The Mitsubishi J8M1 *Shushi* short-range interceptor was based broadly on the Messerschmitt Me 163B. Like the volatile Me 163, the first prototype crashed shortly after takeoff on July 7, 1945.

This Nakajima J1N1-S *Gekko* "Irving" night fighter is the world's last remaining J1N1 airframe. Transported from Japan, it was briefly flight-tested by the USAAF in 1946 and shortly after put into storage. It can now be seen at the National Air and Space Museum. NATIONAL MUSEUM OF THE USAF

The J1N1 *Gekko* was originally designed as a long twin-engine escort fighter for operations in China. The advent of the A6M Zero-sen, however, pushed the J1N1 into other roles, ending with the night-fighter version created in 1944. Just 470 *Gekkos* were built. NATIONAL MUSEUM OF THE USAF

A Yokosuka P1Y1 *Ginga* "Frances" over the U.S. fleet during the battle for Okinawa. Fast and hard to intercept, the *Ginga* was one of Japan's best late-war designs, but like most Japanese types it would be used as a kamikaze during the Okinawa campaign.

This gun-camera image from an F6F Hellcat shows a Yokosuka D4Y2 *Suisei* "Judy" just before the aircraft is shot down off Okinawa. This D4Y2 is powered by an inline water-cooled Atsuta 32 engine, a copy of the German DB 601.

On April 12, 1945, four Ki-51 "Sonias" were destroyed by the Fireflies of No. 1770 NAS. This gun-camera image captures the demise of one of the four Japanese aircraft. VIA ANDREW THOMAS

A JNAF Mitsubishi G4M2A Model 24 *Otsu* photographed at Clark Field in the Philippines in early 1945. The *Otsu* series was an up-gunned version of the G4M with a long-barreled Type 99 Mark 2 cannon in the dorsal turret and 20mm guns in the waist positions; a 7.7mm gun remained in the nose.

Wrecked JAAF aircraft at Yokosuka Airfield in August 1945. Allied air attacks on Japanese home island airfields were devastating. These aircraft are riddled with shrapnel holes from numerous near misses. In the photo are two Ki-46 "Dinah" planes, a Ki-61, and the cockpit section of a Ki-43.

A close-up of the MK4U-A *Kasei* 26a engine attached to a Mitsubishi J2M5 Raiden. This airframe was part of an underground production line discovered at Oya. Only thirty or forty J2M5s were completed before the end of the war.

This cockpit of the Yokosuka MXY7 *Ohka* rocket flying bomb was found at Atsugi Airfield, 1945. With just enough instruments for a one-way trip, the *Okha* was deployed too late to have any tactical or strategic effect.

American ground crew run up one engine on their captured Kawasaki Ki-45 *Toryu* "Nick." This one is heavily armed with a Ho-203 37mm semiautomatic cannon, which was used in both antibomber and antishipping roles.

A close-up of the Ho-203 37mm cannon. Fed from a twenty-five-round magazine, it had a rate of fire of 120 rounds per minute. Muzzle velocity was 1,890 feet per second.

TECHNICAL AIR INTELLIGENCE CENTER
U.S. NAVAL AIR STATION
ANACOSTIA (20), D.C.

<u>BETTY CARRYING ROCKET PROPELLED PILOTED BOMB</u>

This gun-camera sequence records the final moments of a Japanese Mitsubishi G4M2E carrying an *Ohka* rocket-powered glide bomb. This was one of eighteen "Betty" planes launched on March 21, 1945, during the first *Jinrai* ("Divine Thunder") sortie armed with the *Ohka*. Intercepted by the Hellcats of VF-17 and VBF-17, all eighteen were shot down within twenty minutes.

A Mitsubishi Ki-51 "Sonia" light bomber is shot down by a Hellcat pilot near Okinawa on April 3, 1945. Obsolete by 1945, the "Sonia" was used extensively as a kamikaze.

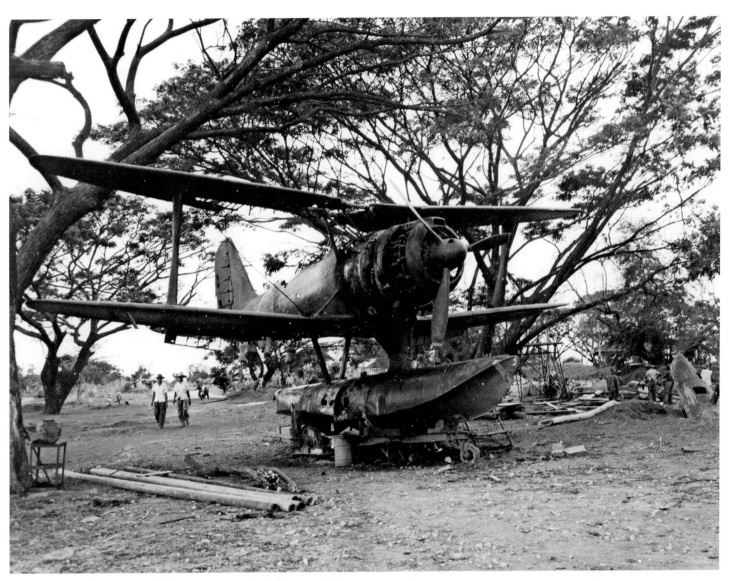

A wrecked Mitsubishi F1M "Pete" floatplane abandoned at Sangley Point in the Philippines. By 1945 most Japanese floatplane, seaplane, bomber, and transport pilots were transferred to either kamikaze units or fighter squadrons assigned to the home defense of Japan.

The Nakajima C6N1-S *Saiun* "Myrt" was considered by many to be one of the finest carrier-based reconnaissance aircraft of the war. Entering service in September 1944, the "Myrt" was used as a high-altitude reconnaissance aircraft. Intercepting fighters had a hard time catching the sleek, pencil-thin aircraft. By 1945 a number of C6N1s had been modified as night fighters, with the remainder used as kamikazes.

Lost in the hail of bursting flak, smoke, and spray from near misses, a solitary Zero-sen skims the wave tops and roars toward the battleship USS *Missouri*. The twin 5-inch gun turret has its guns pointed straight at the oncoming Zero. The attack took place on April 11, 1945, during the Battle of Okinawa. The Zero made it through the gunfire, striking the battleship on its starboard side. There were no American casualties.

BIBLIOGRAPHY

AFF: Official World War II Guide to the Army Air Forces. New York: Bonanza Books, 1988 (reprint of 1944 edition).

Atkinson, Rick. *An Army at Dawn.* New York: Henry Holt and Company, 2002.

Bowan, Martin W. *USAF Handbook: 1939–1945.* Mechanicsburg, PA: Stackpole Books, 1997.

Bridgman, Leonard. *Jane's Fighting Aircraft of World War II.* New Jersey: Crescent Books, 1994.

Carter, William, and Spencer Dunmore. *Reap the Whirlwind: The Untold Story of 6 Group, Canada's Bomber Force of World War II.* Toronto: McClelland and Stewart, Inc., 1991.

Clark, R. Wallace. *British Aircraft Armament, Volume 1: RAF Gun Turrets from 1914 to the Present Day.* Somerset, UK: Patrick Stephens Limited, 1993.

Donald, David, ed. *American Warplanes of World War II.* London: Aerospace Publishing Ltd., 1995.

———. *Warplanes of the Luftwaffe.* London: Aerospace Publishing Ltd., 1994.

English, Allan D. *The Cream of the Crop.* Montreal: McGill-Queen's University Press, 1996.

Ethell, Jeffrey L., et al. *Great Book of World War II Airplanes.* 12 vols. New York: Bonanza Books, 1984.

Everitt, Chris, and Martin Middlebrook. *The Bomber Command War Diaries.* London: Penguin Books, 1990.

Freeman, Roger A. *B-17 Fortress at War.* New York: Charles Scribner's Sons, 1977.

Greenhouse, Brereton, Steven J. Harris, William C. Johnston, and William G. P. Rawling. *The Crucible of War 1939–1945: The Official History of the Royal Canadian Air Force, Volume III.* Toronto: University of Toronto Press, Inc., 1994.

Gunston, Bill. *Classic World War II Aircraft Cutaways.* London: Osprey Publishing, 1995.

Halliday, Hugh A. *Typhoon and Tempest: The Canadian Story.* Toronto: CANAV Books, 1992.

Hardesety, Von. *Red Phoenix: The Rise of Soviet Air Power, 1914–1945.* Washington D.C.: Smithsonian Institution, 1982.

Hogg, Ian V. *The Guns: 1939–45.* New York: Ballantine Books Inc., 1970.

Holmes, Tony. *Hurricane Aces, 1939–40.* Oxford: Osprey Publishing, 1998.

Jarrett, Philip, ed. *Aircraft of the Second World War.* London: Putnam Aeronautical Books, 1997.

Kaplan, Philip, and Jack Currie. *Round the Clock.* New York: Random House, Inc., 1993.

Lake, Jon. *Halifax Squadrons of World War 2.* Oxford: Osprey Publishing, 1999.

March, Daniel J. *British Warplanes of World War II.* London: Aerospace Publishing Ltd., 1998.

Middlebrook, Martin, and Chris Everitt. *The Bomber Command War Diaries.* London: Penguin Books Ltd., 1990.

Murray, Williamson. *The Luftwaffe, 1933–45: Strategy for Defeat.* Washington D.C.: Brassey's, 1989.

Nijboer, Donald. *Graphic War: The Secret Aviation Drawings and Illustrations of World War II.* Ontario, Canada: The Boston Mills Press, 2005.

O'Leary, Michael. *VIII Fighter Command at War: 'Long Reach'.* Oxford: Osprey Publishing, 2000.

Perkins, Paul. *The Lady.* Charlottesville, VA: Howell Press, 1997.

Price, Alfred. *Aggressors: Patrol Aircraft Vs Submarine.* Charlottesville, VA: Howell Press, 1991.

———. *The Last Year of the Luftwaffe: May 1944 to May 1945.* Minneapolis: Motorbooks, 1991.

———. *The Luftwaffe Data Book.* London: Greenhill Books, 1997.

———. *Luftwaffe Handbook.* New York: Charles Scribner's Sons, 1977.

———. *Spitfire Mark I/II Aces 1939–41.* London: Osprey Publishing, 1996.

Remington, Roger R. *American Modernism: Graphic Design, 1920–1960.* New Haven, CT: Yale University Press, 2003.

Sakaida, Henry. *Imperial Japanese Navy Aces 1937–45.* London: Osprey Publishing, 1998.

Scutts, Jerry. *German Night Fighter Aces of World War 2.* Oxford: Osprey Publishing, 1998.

Shores, Christopher, and Chris Thomas. *2nd Tactical Air Force.* Vols. I–IV. Surrey, UK: Classic Publications, 2004, 2005, 2006, and 2008.

Weal, John. *Bf 109F/G/K Aces of the Western Front.* Oxford: Osprey Publishing, 1999.

Williamson, Murray. *The Luftwaffe, 1933–45: Strategy for defeat.* Washington, D.C.: Brassey's, 1996.

PERIODICALS

Buttler, Tony. "Database: de Havilland Mosquito." *Aeroplane* (November 2000).

Eleazer, Wayne. "Supercharged." *Airpower* (November 2001).

———. "Cutaway Kings: Peter Endsleigh Castle." *Aeroplane* (November 1999).

Hall, Tim. "Cutaway Kings: Roy Cross." *Aeroplane* (September 2000).

Mitchell, Fraser-Harry. "Database: Handley Page Halifax." *Aeroplane* (May 2003).

Price, Alfred. "The First Cruise Missile." *Aeroplane* (March 2001).

PUBLIC RECORDS

Air Technical Intelligence Group. *Japanese Aircraft Carrier Operations, Part I.* Report No. 1, October 4 and 5, 1945.

Air Technical Intelligence Group, Advanced Echelon Far East Air Forces, Tokyo, Japan. *Flying Safety in the Japanese Air Forces.* Report No. 251, December 15, 1945.

Air Defence Pamphlet No. 8, "Barrage Balloons," November 1942.

Air Crew Training Bulletin No. 19, August 1944.

Air Crew Training Bulletin No. 22, February 1945.

ACKNOWLEDGMENTS

This book would not be possible without the help and support from the following people and organizations: The Canadian Warplane Heritage Museum, Dan Patterson, Nick Stroud, Tony Holmes, Andrew Thomas, Brett Stolle, Henry Sakaida, Giorgio Apostolo, Barrett Tillman, Frank Mitchell, Phil Listemann, and Gennady Sloutski.